To Mark Davis
...A great servant +
son to me

Jn B III

Unlikely BLESSINGS

Discovering Happiness through the Life of Joseph

JOHN M. BORDERS III

A HIGHLAND HOUSE BOOK
ISBN: 978-1-61868-562-9
ISBN (eBook): 978-1-61868-561-2

UNLIKELY BLESSINGS
Discovering Happiness through the Life of Joseph
© 2015 by John Matthew Borders III
All Rights Reserved

Highland House
109 International Drive, Suite 300
Franklin, TN 37067
http://posthillpress.com

To my wife Sandra, my mother Lille,
Leylana, Matthew, and Brittany, my children, and
Madison and Bailey
My grandchildren

My offering to Jesus Christ

Contents

Profound, Practical, and Precious

Foreword
Kirk Byron Jones

Author of
***Fulfilled**: Living and Leading with Unusual Wisdom, Peace, and Joy*
*and **Refill**: Meditations for a Leading with Wisdom, Peace, and Joy*

The spiritual power of *Unlikely Blessings* has already been affirmed by the tender hearted pastor and curious minded bible study group that gave birth to it. To know this pastor-writer's heart, all you have to do is hear him address his energized and faithful Morning Star Baptist Church family just once as, "Beloved." When Bishop John Borders refers to his church family as such he means it with all his soul; you can hear the love in his voice and feel the love in his spirit. Knowing the unique spiritual authenticity of both pastor and church, my expectations were high as I began reading *Unlikely Blessings*. I was not disappointed.

Unlikely Blessings is a profound book:

"Adversity is not the absence of favor, but the development of it."

"Light does not contend. Light does not fight back. Light shines. Light does not have to prove anything. Light simply shines."

"Any ministry telling you about what you can get and not who you should become is leading you astray."

Unlikely Blessings is a practical book:

"God will often reinforce your dream with other dreams of the same theme, until you have confidence to work them out. When God has a purpose in your life, you will see it unfold in your heart and soul before you live it out."

"Consider this question: "What do you bring when you walk into a room?" When you go home, to work, sit on the bus, walk into the house of God, does anyone know you are there?"

"Part of your worship is to get proper rest."

Unlikely Blessings is a precious book:

"Come to terms with the fact that there is an unusual favor upon your life, and walk in it so that God can bring you to your destiny."

"What was beautiful about Joseph was the glory of God in his life."

"When God opens the windows of heaven for us, blessings chase blessings, and we are not even prepared to receive them all."

We all can use the wisdom of a profound book. When that book happens to have clear relevancy for everyday life and is so divinely soft on the ears and to the soul, to the point of sounding like poetry at times, that is blessing on blessing on blessing. How unlikely, and thoroughly wonderful!

Personally, one of me favorite quotes from *Unlikely Blessings* is, *"The force of spirituality is being who we are on the inside even though our situation denies that."* Perhaps these words, more than any other, capture the central meaning of this meaningful book for me: What's in you is always greater than what's against you.

Acknowledgments

Writing a book has many starts and stops. Momentum builds and it wanes. Many people contribute to the author's work in different seasons. I thank those people for their help and sacrifice.

First, to my wife Sandra: without you I would have nothing to share with the world. I see your face in every great thought and every insightful moment. I have no inspiration without you.

To my mother, for raising me, loving me, and helping me believe. To my father, John M. Borders Jr., thank you for passing down the writing gene. I love you. To my children, Leylana, Matthew, and Brittany, who constantly admonish me to stop comparing myself to others, and frequently ask, "When will you believe in yourself and realize God ordained you for this?" You three are a reminder of what can be accomplished in faith. To Francisca and Brandon, my daughter- and son-in-law, I love you both for the sunshine you've brought to the Borders family. To Madison and Bailey, You're my Joy. Poppa loves you!

To my adopted sons Jamel Davenport (The Mad Trainer) and Joshua Clachar: Jamel, thank you for encouraging me to live a healthy life. Joshua there is so much left to explore in our business and partnership. We have not finished yet.

To Rev. Dr. James Coleman, Rev. Dr. Elliot Mason, Rev. Dr. Frederick G. Sampson, Rev. Dr. Tony C. Campbell, and Rev. Charles C. Taylor; your spirits will live in me forever.

To Archbishops Bailey and Laufers and the International Bishops Conference, I am thankful to God that you are my brothers in the Bishopric.

To the wonderful leadership and congregation of Morning Star Baptist Church in Boston, who support my ministry and encourage me to be a man of God. To Margaret Jean, Tina Wright-Hicks, and Brent Butler, my executive assistants, confidants and friends through the years; I love you.

In the beginning, Kelly Cameron and Hollee Freeman helped give birth to my dream of becoming an author. Ebony Harvey transcribed my bible study lessons during services, which led to this work. Natasha Noel, Naeema Fuller, and Juah Seyonia Washington attended many meetings at Panera Bread. You all helped provide the scaffolding for my dream of writing.

To Byron Pitts, who advised me to lead during tough times in Boston;

to Dr. Lance Watson, who introduced me to some of the greatest church leaders in the world and encouraged me to keep moving forward;

to Dr. Walter E. Fluker and Ambassador Charles Stith for your brotherhood through 30 years of ministry; you pushed me further and gave me room to grow.

To Bishop Joseph and Dr. Stephanie Walker of Mt. Zion Baptist Church and to Johnnie Stephens, you represent stepping stones of faith; to Arch Bishop Leroy Bailey and my colleagues of the International Bishop's Conference Incorporated for welcoming me into the family.

To Dr. Kirk Byron Jones, Rev. Dr. Martha Simmons, Rev. Dr. Kevin Turman, Sharon, LaQuintta Newton, Danita Jo, Douglas Martin Esq., Carmen Santos, Nena Madonia—who taught me the publishing industry and opened doors for me—you are the echo that allows my voice to reach far and wide.

To Dr. Erika Schwartz, my doctor and friend, to Anthony, Gavin and Michael from Post Hill Press for believing in me and for taking publishing in a brand new direction.

My meager thanks is not enough to convey the depth of my gratitude of the importance of our relationships. I cannot remember every individual who encouraged me in this process. God will remember you and bless you for helping me. Yet I will say it again—with a heart full of devotion—thank you!

Introduction

There is a Joseph in every family. He or she is usually the target of jealousy, but is the essential force of the family. He or she is favored by some family members, but generally castigated by others. Joseph has no guile, but is surrounded by beguiling and treacherous circumstances. Joseph is the person who, without any choice of their own, the expectations on their life is higher than that of their family members and friends. Thus, they cannot get away with the same things. By nature Joseph just takes on more. He takes on his problems and the problems of those close to him. Joseph waits longer, he suffers more, he gets criticized more, he works harder, and he has an innate burden to be more responsible than others. If this is you, it's because God composed your personality as such, so that your life will be liberating and affect change in a powerful way.

Your in-laws can be a headache. Husbands and wives are careful about criticizing their spouse's family. You try to be supportive and agreeable with your spouse as you listen to the sad or sometimes boring stories of irresponsibility or petty squabbles going on in the family. Everyone has the proverbial "Black Sheep," the "Don Juan," the "Jezebel," and the "Mother Hubbard." It does not matter if the family is rich or poor, blue-blooded or blue collar; there is always family drama.

There is at least one person in the family to whom everyone else confides in about family drama. Add family drama with drama at work or school, or church…and a pattern emerges. You feel responsible to address the problems or assume blame for most of the family's drama. One day I was listening to my wife discuss some family drama. We've been married over 25 years so I had heard it many times before. She has heard my complaints about family issues to an equal amount; I listened patiently like all supportive husbands. Suddenly, God's presence overshadowed me. I understood my wife as never before. I knew why she felt so strongly about the problems in her family, why she took on so much, and why her siblings always called upon her even though she was the second youngest.

I saw a spiritual headlight shining a path on her entire life. The Lord changed my understanding of who I was married to that instant. I was sitting next to a person of destiny, someone who possessed greater grace and strength than she realized. Her frustrations were real but they did not tell the future. Sandra was coming into a season of great blessing. She is Joseph. I couldn't contain myself. I told her the story of Joseph and his brothers. She listened with new interest as the story replicated her life and sentiments. "You are Joseph!" I said to her. Sandra looked at me as if she had had an "ah-ha moment." Without saying anything, she nodded in agreement with a sense of peace about the entire matter.

Beyond all doubt, I know I am married to a person like Joseph.

I then taught on Joseph for over 20 weeks during Wednesday Edification at Morning Star Baptist Church. Those Wednesday evenings enriched our spirits. We couldn't wait to dig into the Word the following Wednesday. We studied the Bible, but I shared my reflections, life principles, and inspiration too. Many nights the Holy Spirit gave us new insights and inspiration regarding Joseph's life. The Anointing flowed like a river and people gained a new sense of self-esteem as the weeks flew by.

My preparation for each class took me deep into study. I did not search for the sake of scholarship, but for living principles. I was transformed by each study period and even more by sharing my reflections with the church. Several hundred people studied, laughed, cried, stood on their feet and applauded, and prayed earnestly every Wednesday night - hoping the Joseph story would not end. By the time we came to Joseph's disclosure of who he was, that he did not die in the desert but was the chief administrator of Egypt, we were changed as a class. We experienced new insights into leadership, love, and reconciliation. The Joseph story builds into the remarkable scene of 70 members of Jacob's clan packing up their belongings and moving away from the poverty and famine of Canaan to the robust and abundant supply of grain in Egypt. Every Joseph is destined to bring about lasting and significant change for themselves and others. Joseph's life points to a climaxing season where it all works together for a greater good.

There are three major questions every Joseph asks:

Why is my life so difficult?

Why must I always be the responsible one?

When will it be my turn?

Unlikely Blessings will attempt to address these questions with you. This is not a book for speed-readers. You should not rush through these pages because time is required to reflect on Joseph's story and compare your life to his. Watch for parallels as you read each page, when asking, "Why is my life so difficult?"

You will better understand what it means to be blessed when you read the CHAPTER on "What Does Happy Means." We all have dreams of success and achievement. Also, we see visions and tell stories in our dreams. A spiritual excitement will come upon you as you read the section on "Dreams." You will see the importance of maintaining integrity in the CHAPTER on the "Sacred Trust." You will gain inspiration from the "The Sacred Space of Prison."

We all get dismayed at times. When you read, "Sent in the Wrong Direction for the Right Reasons," you will resolve that God is in control of your life and circumstances. There may be no greater story of inspiration for you than Joseph's story. If you take in what you read and apply it to your life, you be in awe by Unlikely Blessings.

Chapter 1
WHAT DOES HAPPY MEAN?

Psalm 128

In the Joseph account, Joseph's troubles are unlikely to lead to blessings, but they do. This book is an attempt to show the progressive stages of blessings. These days, the generation of people in their 20s get things fast and don't know what it's like to "pay their dues" or work for things. The life of Joseph falls into three stages: *adversity, challenges,* and *leadership.* Adversities can break your spirit and kill your dreams. You think God abandoned you to wither away in exile. Yet you survive. When destiny arrives you find yourself with more responsibility. God doesn't manufacture selfish blessings; the more blessed you are the more you're responsible for. We must learn to focus on the journey and not the circumstances. All the events of life have meaning. We should always ask God, "What does this mean for me now as well as later?" Favor brings antagonism and you become a threat. The moment your life is more exposed to influence, favor, and responsibility, the more you will make people uncomfortable and they will be willing to highlight your flaws. Adversity is not the absence of favor but the development of it. Promotion is often sudden and expected in the *Kairos* moment. (Kairos means "the perfect moment" in ancient Greek.) You will be unprepared for the swiftness with which your life changes. However, you'll look back and see the Master Craftsman shaped you for destiny when your life began. This lesson is for people who want to make a difference for the Kingdom. Joseph was anointed in the pit, in the prison, and in Potiphar's house. Anointed is who you are, not what you do. Patience is the key to blessing.

Psalm 40. "I rested while I waited" for God. Do you want God to give you the Kingdom when you are not prepared for it? Men and women who are called to greatness must never be vengeful. No matter what a person does to you they cannot stop what God is doing. They cannot smother the anointing nor slow you down. If we are vengeful, we will tarnish the blessings that lie ahead. God will "teach you to forget your afflictions." The Hebrew word *Manasseh* means learning to forget. In the Old Testament (OT), it is a manner of looking back on life and seeing God's hand at every turn. What would you be if you had not gone through the trials you did? When you recognize you are the blessed of God simple things become sources and evidence of God's blessing. Appreciation for the simple things in life is the key to being blessed. A blessed, anointed life has the depth of relationships. People care about you, care what happens to you, and care when you are happy or sad. Relationships are not superficial and your life becomes more vital to other people. Blessedness draws people. A blessed life has inner peace and contentment. You learn to be happy with the little that you have. When you're blessed of God and have no job, you're still blessed of God. You have peace and you know that God will provide for all your needs. A blessed life is carried by fortitude.

You will not be blessed of God if you do not work hard. The hand of the diligent shall rule. Seek and ye shall find, ask and it shall be given, knock and the door will be open to you. You will feel like quitting, but will not be able to. A blessed life makes sound decisions, does not panic, and never claims the victim. The Hebrew word E'esher is translated as happy or blessed and comes from the name Asher [Genesis 30:9-13]. In the New Testament (NT) the idea of being happy or blessed is different [Matthew 5:3]. It is not a matter of conditional happiness; it is a declaration of one's identity. It is not a matter of looking for the blessing or waiting for someone to tell you you are blessed. You declare the promises of God over your life.

Isaiah 32:20: "Blessed are you when you sow beside all waters."[The World English Bible] This is a picture of someone who owns a piece of land which has been flooded. Instead of complaining, you say to yourself, "the sun will shine and this water will dry up, so I am going to plant seeds in the flood and the harvest will come." Blessed is the person who can look at a situation and see the future.

Chapter 2
DREAMS

Anytime a parent favors a child more than others, it is apparent the child is favored. Any parent who sets that precedent leads that child to trouble. The coat represented his favor and anointing, but Joseph was also a tattletale. The coat of many colors was possibly more like his father making him a coat of materials which he had not used for any coat previously.

All of us dream and remember some of them. Our dreams tell us we are spiritual and we exist in more than one realm of reality. Dreams are like unusual interruptions of reality. Dreams have color; they are long or short, funny or scary. There are dreams we want to continue and dreams we want to forget. God spoke to various individuals like Daniel and Peter through dreams.

What function do dreams have? Hobson and McCarley suggested that dreams "are not without psychological meaning and function." The significance of the dream narrative, in Hobson's present view, comes only after the powerful neurochemical perimeters are set and interpreted by the higher-order parts of the brain that deal with language, logic and the mapping of emotions with remembered experiences.[1]

During sleep our brain goes on safari and runs away, allowing itself to heal from the stresses of life that occurred earlier that day. If we don't allow our brain the "freedom to become undisciplined" during sleep, it will affect our emotions, reactions, thought processes, and life. When this happens – for some people - they dream allegorical dreams; stories that are connected to their reality or someone else's reality. They are so profound and clear they require interpretation. This is close to what happened to Joseph. If his brothers already hated him why did he run up to his them to share his dreams? It was so profound that he must have desired interpretation. Caveat: Be careful who you share your dreams

---

1   Allan Hobson and R. McCarley, The Brain as a Dream State Generator: an Activation-Synthesis Hypothesis," American Journal of Psychiatry 134 (1977), 1335-1348.

and revelations with. Not everything God shares with you should be shared with others.

Some dreams tell us our future. They are given by God and give us direction or a hint of the plans that he has for us. Other dreams are "waking dreams." They are the aspirations we have when we are awake which force us to struggle with our purpose. Every one of us needs to deal with the fact that there is a dream or aspiration in our life which is given to us from God and if we are smart, focused, and obedient, we should pursue it. Martin Luther King, Jr. had aspirations of ending racism so high they became his life's message and defined his role on earth. Waking dreams are connected to subconscious dreams, which occur in rapid eye movement (REM) sleep. They are so important to our destiny they play out in our unconscious state.

Every person who understands that there is within them a spark to do some significance is plagued by the fault of their missteps to get there. The job of the ministry is to help that person coax that spark to a flame. Joseph goes to his brothers, tells them about his dreams and they get upset. Some dreams are directly from God and are so important that to ignore them is to suffer (either waking or subconscious). Imagine what would have happened if Joseph never told his dreams, if all these bad things happened, but he had no handle to understand them? What would have happened to his father, brothers and the 70 others who came to Egypt to inevitably become the nation of Israel? What would have happened if Joseph had suppressed the dream when the angel told him to flee to Egypt with Mary and Jesus? What would have happened if Peter had ignored the dream of all kinds of animals coming down on the white sheet?

In Verse 8, "They hated him all the more for his dream and what he had said." Joseph attached his dream to his conversation. Why have a vision and not attach it to your conversation? Imagine walking along the way and something grabs you and you ignore it and keep doing what you're doing. Then it grabs you again, but now you are fearful and you run like Jonah. Your life begins to crumble and right before it falls apart, it grabs you again, but this time you say: "Since I can't run from it, I can't run from The Almighty." Once again it grabs you and you begin to speak to your friends and family about the fears of walking in this thing.

It is time for you not to be afraid to live out what you have seen in your spirit from the Holy Spirit.

Some of you have been called by God to change the status quo, to change the norm, to confront religion and bring a fresh breeze of God's presence back to starving millions and millions of people, who are waiting to see if anyone knows the Lord. And you wish that you could walk away from it.

Grab hold of these admonitions.

Live with the fact that great dreams and significant dreams will make people think you are arrogant. They will call you arrogant because you dare to believe in God. Do not cower, do not apologize, do not back up. Joseph had to deal with the fact that his brothers hated him.

Dreams that are connected with your future need one thing to be lived out: obedience. If God has placed a dream in your spirit, it will come as it will come. You don't have to do anything different. You do not have to help a dream.

There are dreams and then there are visions. The dreams that are visions are given to you to help you see the purpose of your life. Joseph's dream showed him that he would be prime minister to a nation.

Put your friends in categories. Some friends you pour into, some pour into you, and some cause drag. Share your visions with people who pour into your life.

Dreams that are also visions reveal the fact that God has given you dominion and authority. When we think of the anointing of the Lord in our lives we think influence; we think high, instead of thinking low. May the anointing of God on your life be so great that you become invisible, that you become nothing. If the Lord has given you authority, i.e. designed you to lead, don't apologize. Because it's not about you—it's about larger numbers. He didn't give you the gift to say, "Look how great I am." He gave it so you can be low and serve others.

Do not forget the images in your dreams because they are tied to the events of the future. Joseph dreamed about *sheaths* connected to how he would save Egypt.

Let the feelings you have about your "crazy dreams" motivate you to go out and pursue a higher calling. If they are in you what are you doing about it? People don't change the status of their lives because they don't take any actions regarding the status of their dreams based on what they believe.

Sometimes others can have dreams about you to reinforce your purpose. Sometimes there will be grace on your life in such a way people will call you and tell you about it because you need to hear it then. In Judges 7, God tells Gideon that he needs to take a nation down with 300 soldiers. To take down a nation of 300,000! God answers a series of tests for Gideon's comfort and God gives one more assurance to Gideon. A man was telling a dream to a companion, "A loaf of barley bread came into the camp of Midian and the tent collapsed." A piece of bread brought down an army (verse 9). When Gideon heard the dream and the interpretation, he was ready to go.

God will often reinforce your dream with other dreams of the same theme until you have confidence to work them out. When God has a purpose in your life you will see it unfold in your heart and soul before you live it out.

You can't tell everyone your dreams because some can't handle it. When God tells Abraham to sacrifice Isaac, he doesn't tell Sarah. Abraham tells her they are going to worship.

Don't be afraid of great dreams. But be afraid of not accepting them and denying them. The harm is for God to show you something about yourself, someone else, or the world, and you ignore it. That is a sin.

Chapter 3
SENT IN THE WRONG DIRECTION FOR THE RIGHT REASONS

Gen 37:12-36

It's one thing to see your life drifting away and falling apart when you're in Sin, but it's another thing to see your life drifting away and falling apart when you're in God's Will. On your way to your destiny there are sad seasons and moments in life. No one who has ever been anointed and blessed by God has avoided going through a sad season. It seems that once the announcement is made that you are God's chosen the Spirit leads you directly into the wilderness. Joseph went farther away from home, further into danger and further into God's will. The only way we will find out what God has for us is to end up in a place where we are removed from all things familiar. Joseph goes from Hebron to Sichem to Dothan to Egypt. He is far away from home.

Hebron is the place where Abram built an altar to God; it was the land where Joseph's grandfather was blessed, where the people walked in favor. It was safe like your home church. The brothers were feeding the herds in Sichem, about 60 miles away—a 30-hour journey—because the land was lush. The brothers were going to nurse the flocks there for a while, maybe even weeks. No wonder the father said, "Where are my sons and the flocks?" And he then sent for Joseph. Joseph was willing to go find his brothers, but naïve to what lay ahead. Recall that the brothers were envious of Joseph because he had the father's favor and he tattled on them.

As Joseph was arriving, the brothers saw him from far-off and decided to kill him. Time had passed and they were still angry, they had not let it go. Whenever God tries to deliver us from hate, anger, or bitterness, the devil constantly tries to remind us why we are angry and keep us there. When Joseph got to Sichem he found the brothers had gone to Dotham, the place of two wells. Note that in this time you did not send your flocks to graze on someone else's land. When Jacob sent them 60 miles away he still owned the land because God had blessed him so. Joseph was naïve walking toward his brothers because he did not remember their anger against him. There is a sense of naïveté in the Holy Spirit. When people are walking in the flesh they are cunning, but people in the Spirit are trusting in God; they do not worry about fighting their own battles because they are trusting the Lord to take care of them [cp *Matthew 10:16*]. Jesus is saying, "I am sending you into deceitfulness and I want you to bring my word to the snakes and the vipers in threatening territory. Remember that everyone has an agenda and not everyone is telling the truth. You will be sheep in the midst of wolves but you cannot become a wolf."

We are adaptable; if we are in the midst of wolves we will act like a wolf [cp *Philippians 2:14, 15*]. Become blameless and harmless children of God without fault in the midst of a perverse generation. You are responsible for what you do, so you can't live any way you want to fit in with the people around you. Joseph walks in the midst of his brothers conspiring to take his life. They say, "The master of dreams is coming, let's kill him." This is a disturbing statement because for the brothers to call Joseph the "master of dreams" was to imply he had a connection with heaven that they did not. It was to imply that as he went through life he was getting instruction from a deity, and it is a statement of blasphemy. They wanted to kill him because he had an unusual spirit.

When God's grace is on your life you don't have to open your mouth to convict others, you just make them uncomfortable. When someone is walking in the spirit, the world will accuse you of being deceitful and demonic. As we walk through the life of Joseph, we see the life of Jesus. Joseph is being persecuted because he had an unusual spirit. The religious people wanted to kill Jesus because he had an unusual spirit. If he would have joined the Pharisees or Sadducees they would not have been concerned about him. Come to terms with the fact there is an unusual favor upon your life and walk in it so God can bring you to your destiny.

The brothers and Joseph were in Dotham, a two or three days journey away, so whatever they decided to say they had enough time to convince the group they can carry out the lie. No matter how far you go away to sin when you get home, the same conviction will follow. When you think God is not watching or listening, the walls and ground will speak and bear witness to your nefarious ways.

They throw their brother in a pit and sit to eat lunch. Thank God for Reuben, the oldest brother with a conscious. He recognizes the fact that he will have to give an account of his brother. But Joseph was sold when Reuben went away. It parallels to when Pontius Pilate tries to appease the crowd when they wanted to crucify Jesus. He offered to scourge him but it was not enough. Throwing Joseph in the pit was not enough, they wanted to kill him or sell him.

Thank God for your near misses, the times in your life when you should have died, but didn't. Those Reuben-esque moments in your life when you should have been wiped out but God gave you another chance. You are not as strong or as spiritual as you wish you were but at least you are still here, not doing what you used to do. Thank God! Thank God for compassion on someone's heart concerning you. When Satan plans for destruction there is one way out—God.

Chapter 4
PEOPLE WHO ENTER YOUR LIFE, CHANGE IT

Genesis 39: 1-6

We want to see how Joseph's life and spirit interconnect with ours. We have a simple but paramount subject in Joseph's story. Consider this question: "What do you bring when you walk into a room?" When you go home, to work, sit on the bus, walk into the house of God, does anyone know you are there? Not just from knowing your name or that you are the "cousin/brother/wife of". But when you go out, is your private life such that when you go out in public your presence is felt? Does your being here enhance the Kingdom? When you give your life to Jesus Christ and you begin to grow, you begin to radiate and emit the presence of God as Jesus said, "let your light shine before men…." [Matthew 5:16]

You begin to emanate Jesus Christ a little more in your life and Jesus begins to trust you to bring back the correct change in the currency of his Kingdom. The Lord begins to give you more and you start to influence more. Then you are given more responsibility and you grow more, and become more of an evangelist and you grow more, and so on. You get concerned about people and their problems and their growth. You begin to see God start doing things before you even ask. You go further and you meet men and women of God whom you admire. Then they begin to admire you in your spiritual life. You go further after that and you begin to recognize who you are spiritually and what it means for you to be in a particular place. Then your spiritual life begins to affect the atmosphere around you. Remember the Seven Sons of Sceva (Acts 19)? They tried to exorcise a demon but were unable because they did not walk in the power of the Spirit. What the demons were saying was "We know Paul and Jesus because their spirit affects the atmosphere, but your spirit does not." Look at the spiritual life like this: at one level of spiritual growth God affects you, but as you continue to grow you begin to affect your family and friends, then your neighbors, a city, the region, etc. This is "The Circumference of Blessing."

When God wants to do something in a certain city God will go to gatekeepers. It will be revealed to some so they can be instrumental in carrying out the revelation to the body of Christ. These gatekeepers have more influence than just their local congregation. When Joseph walked in the room, things changed. When Joseph walked into Potiphar's house, his house became more successful. When Joseph went into prison after being accused of rape, the jail's atmosphere changed. The relationships between God and the prisoners changed. Greater efficiency was taking place among the tasks just because Joseph showed up.

What happens in a room when you show up? Do people mock your spirituality? Say, "That's a member of Morning Star?" Say, "He does this" or "She does that?" Or, when you walk in a room do people feel convicted? Inspired? Do they sense the Holy Spirit? Have a desire to seek the face of God just because you showed up?

My grandfather John M Borders Sr. was a television repairman. He knew everything about Philco, Zenith, and RCA televisions. His storefront on Franklin Avenue in Brooklyn, New York, was piled high with transistors, vacuum tubes, and Radiola speakers and picture tubes. I used to go with him to jobs where I learned how to repair and work televisions and radios. Now whenever I go to a place where there is a broken down television I must repair it. I cannot leave it broken down. I cannot go into a person's life, who is going through challenges, and not take some ownership enough to pour into their lives; to offer spiritual counseling and to pray for them because I can't go into a place and not affect it.

The reason why I will not go into a place and not affect it is that I have to: (1) survive, so I need to go into the room and know who is in there, who I am dealing with; and (2) because my assignment as a pastor and spiritual leader is understanding that everyone, man or woman, is flawed and everyone needs Jesus as Lord and Savior. I have to start to discern what God is doing and pray for grace in order to affect change in the situation. But what do you bring when you walk in a room? Does the devil know you are there? Did the Holy Spirit walk in the room because you walked in it? Is the family better because you are a member of it? Do you have a sanctifying force on your life, whether you announce it or not, that is changing the atmosphere? Do they want to fire you at your job or give you a promotion? Do they want to make sure they keep you because the margins of profitability have gone up because you are in the room? That is what is happening in Genesis 39. Before we get to Potiphar's wife's accusations we must look at what happened to Potiphar because of Joseph. CHAPTER 37 ends with Jacob believing that Joseph is dead because of the brother's lie, but Joseph had been sold into slavery and eventually sold to Potiphar, Captain of the Guard. The story picks back up in CHAPTER 39.

No one who comes into your life just comes along. No one in your life is there by accident, whether it is for good or ill. No one just shows up; it is a matter of divine timing. When God is in it, people are sent before you at a strategic time. Just as when the Ishmaelite traders came to pass where Joseph was in the pit. They had come down that pass many times but this time God had ordained they would buy him for slavery and further his destiny. When God tells you that you are blessed or your blessing is coming in the future, God does not reveal the details of how that blessing will be processed. Because if you knew the details you would run in the other direction and say, "This is not a blessing."

When you pray for strength you go through a whirlwind of a storm. Theodicy says you have to do this to get your prayer answered. Joseph had a dream that he would be exulted over his family but God could not tell him that he had to be put in the pit and sold into slavery before he was placed in Pharaoh's court. No one just comes into your life. Everyone has a role: a function, a story, an insight to bring, a burden to share, a love to create, a problem to solve a lesson to disclose, a hand to offer in your way to bring significance into your life. If someone in your life now has brought you pain, you need to ask God, "What is the lesson, the message behind this pain that I am experiencing initiated by this person? Are you trying to change something, initiate something? Did you send them to me so that I can buffer them?"

Potiphar means devoted to the sun or Sun God. He was an Egyptian, raised in Egyptian culture, so he did not know anything about the God of Abraham, Isaac and Jacob. His god was Ra, the sun god of Egypt. He was a heathen. He did not believe in the true and living God. He was a polytheist. He was the Captain of the Guard, so Potiphar was a killer. The Young's Literal translation of the Bible says "Potiphar was the Head of the Executioners." He worked his way up in Pharaoh's court because he was a brutal man, but he was wise and he became an instrument of God for the children of Israel. He saw Joseph was young and strong and he needed another house servant. So Potiphar bought him. Potiphar also received a tap on his shoulder from a God he did not know who said, "buy him."

When you are in the spirit of God, when God is with you, people who do not believe in your God find themselves influenced to show you favor and consideration. When a man or woman says "the favor of God is on my life" what they are saying is doors open up for them by people they are not associated with for some unknown reason only they know of. That God is the one opening doors saying yes and causing non-Christians to bless you and help you along the way. They don't even realize that the Holy Ghost had worked in the atmosphere to lead them to show you favor at that particular time. For some reason Potiphar buys this slave that touches his life. He studies him and gives him authority in his house, and as Joseph begins to work everything in Potiphar's house changes for the better. With all the things that Potiphar was responsible for he is now making more profit. Things that were in disarray are now in order because Joseph is there.

Potiphar was a brutal man. Potiphar was a man of great influence in Egypt. Potiphar was a heathen who served a false God. Potiphar was a stranger to Joseph and God ordained that Joseph would live with him. God sent Joseph to live with a heathen. Don't miss it. Joseph is living in a household and town where Yahweh is not a consideration at all. He has no spiritual support at all in the town. He has to bring God into the situation. He cannot go into the situation expecting to be encouraged. He is alone with his God and God sent him there to live. Just in case you are living with a heathen; just in case you are living in a region where there is nothing but pain, pressure, tension, reefer smoking, drugs, alcohol, arguing, cursing, this and that. Instead of saying, "Oh Lord, take me out," pray, "Lord, while I am here, I'm going to bring Jesus Christ to such an effect that when I leave the heathens in the house will know you as Lord and Savior." When Joseph walked in the room everything in the room was blessed.

God handpicked Potiphar to become Joseph's master. While God handpicked him, he is one step away from Pharaoh. But the reason why Potiphar's house was blessed and the reason why Joseph began to thrive in the house of a heathen is because Joseph walked in the house as a godly man. Godliness is something we don't talk about a whole lot in the house of God. We talk a lot about the anointing but not about godliness. The right arm of the anointing is godliness. There is no anointing without godliness. There is no anointing of the Holy Spirit on a person who says, "I'm gifted, I'm touched by God and I can live any way that I want." There is no anointing on that life.

It's like making a cake, getting the best ingredients to make the cake. The cake is perfect. You sit it on the table and the family is getting ready to eat it and there is a roach on the cake. When people are expecting godliness and they find something else, it's like buying outdated bread. Don't say you have the anointing of the Holy Spirit and yet you are not godly. Don't say the Spirit of God is great upon your life when you are not striving every day to live in the holiness and righteousness of God through Jesus Christ. Godliness is reverence of God that causes a person to live according to the highest moral and ethical standards they can and they live their lives with due diligence. You cannot ignore that Joseph was a hard worker. Anyone who wants to be successful or great must work hard. It will not just come because the prophet spoke over your life. That is not how God does it. God does it by seed and season. He does it by the laws of righteousness, godliness, faith, and truth. That is how a man or woman is blessed. That is the only way it will last. Godliness is the determination that wherever I am, my mind is going to be on the things of God and I'm going to do what pleases God.

The standard is not my peers, the standard is the Lord. I'm going to work hard because I'm pleasing him.

When godliness happens in you the whole atmosphere changes. In 1 Timothy 4:8 it says practice being godly. Give yourself to godly things. When you fall short, discipline yourself to do what is right in the sight of God. Building yourself up in godliness, holiness, and righteousness benefits you in every area of your life. It benefits you right now here on earth and in the world to come. When a person decides to do that they will begin to prosper because it is a divine law. God will bless the righteous. God will bless those who seek him first. God will bless those who live in a heathen situation and hold onto their faith. Joseph goes into Potiphar's house and the whole thing changes because Joseph is godly. Godliness is the right arm of the anointing and you cannot be godly and be lazy. Godly people work hard. Godliness brings prosperity to others. When you are a godly man or woman, don't worry about money. Those things will come to you. Concern yourself with godliness and you will never have to worry about money or prosperity, if you concern yourself with being godly.

A godly man or woman will have such influence on an institution or system or family that people in that institution or system or family will succeed and be blessed. If you are truly a godly person people in your life can surpass some of your heart's desires just because you touch their lives. They can receive the things you want because the things you want are actually too small for the shoes you will fill. The things God has for you, because your godliness is so great, you will have to wait for God to bring you in the Kingdom instead of holding onto the desires your family members receive because of you. That is when Paul says godliness is contentment. If you are seeking God and people around you get blessed, as your life gets harder that is because yours did not come yet. What God has for you is tied to the godliness placed inside of you. People are prospering, the systems are becoming more efficient, the atmosphere is becoming more cooperative, and life is still hard for you because when he finally raises up Joseph, Joseph will live on a tier that is beyond his imagination.

Godly people live in the assurance of God's presence. The Holy Spirit aids the godly in every aspect of life and under all circumstances. The Holy Spirit means more to you in daily use, in common situations, and on ordinary days. That is the key to the Holy Spirit. It means more with daily use. The Holy Spirit wants to abide with you when you are having that morning coffee or tea, when you are washing clothes or the car, when you are at work or at school, so that when you need him you've got enough stored up to see deliverance take place on the highest level. Don't live your life any way you want to, not acknowledging the presence of the Holy Spirit, then get in trouble and look for Him to be with you. The Holy Spirit wants to be with you when you are in the grocery line, the unemployment line, and be there fully utilized in the common, ordinary situations. The Holy Spirit is present in our lives, but we don't know it or recognize it. It is not just about speaking in tongues. If you are looking for the Holy Ghost or to understand the Holy Ghost, don't look in Acts, look in Isaiah. For example, Isaiah 61, "The spirit of the Lord is upon me, because he has anointed me to teach good tidings to the poor…." Isaiah 40:28-3 talks about the Holy Spirit. No tongues are mentioned. "But they that wait reverently and in faith upon God shall mount up on wings as eagles."

In the world, I smoked reefer every day in my youth, but I learned that reefer was counterfeit. If you are looking for any stimulation to get high, instead turn to the Holy Spirit. The Holy Spirit will give you a high without guilt, bondage, or hangover. You can speak in tongues and miss heaven but you will not miss heaven if you are godly. You will not miss heaven if you say to yourself "I am a man or woman of God." Pray and ask the Lord what is your purpose. Why you are here. What changes will take place because you are in the room. One more thing about Joseph, he is the administrator of the house of Potiphar because God is training him so he will know how to administer in Pharaoh's house. Sometimes God will give you a small capsule of your future. While you are trying to identify who you are and what you are meant to do, you may already see in a small sense what God has in store for you in the future by the way he is using you now.

Chapter 5
THE SACRED TRUST
PART I

Genesis 39

Notice the two parallel designs in the Scripture. Both Potiphar and the chief of the prisoners did not know what was going on in their respective domains because they had committed everything to Joseph.

Joseph was a strikingly handsome man based on Scripture. Every translation says that Joseph was fine. He was beautiful inside as well as outside. Joseph fits the description of any woman's desire for a man. He was handsome and he knew God. He was a man of integrity. But Joseph's attractiveness was only a small part of this diabolical scheme against him, which God allowed to happen. It was important that Joseph wound up in prison so his destiny could be furthered. What if God told you the way he was going to exalt you was to take you to prison? There are seven points from this CHAPTER we will try to look at over the next few lessons in greater detail:

Maintaining virtue and chastity in the face of temptation.

The importance of understanding your responsibility when you have been given a sacred trust.

How to handle yourself when your virtue gets you in trouble or how to handle yourself when you are in trouble for doing the right things. Meaning every Christian ought to be in trouble with someone because of his or her stance for Jesus Christ. Someone ought to be looking for a way to bring you down because they can't stand your light and witness. All Daniel did was pray three times a day but his prayer was so effective that all the governors of Babylon plotted to bring down his prayer life. Elijah was called the "Troubler of Israel," because he was a man of God.

How do you live through slander and false accusation as a Christian? How do you hold your head up when your name has been ruined?

The sacred space of prison. You may be bound in a situation or in a place of difficulty but watch what happens when you can make the place you are living in sacred. Remember when Paul and Silas were in jail and the doors of the prison opened, but none left? It's because the prison became sacred.

Watching God promote you when you should have failed.

Understanding the sense of timing in biblical storytelling and what it is meant to reinforce.

Joseph was handsome, probably a virgin. He was holy and maintained his chastity even though this woman had longing eyes for him. The spirit of lust was on her and it did not leave her, but became self-destructive. She destroyed her own home in an attempt to destroy Joseph's life. Day after day she enticed him. That is what the enemy does, he wants to whittle away at your integrity. It is never the first attempt that will get you, but the call to yield resounding day after day, week after week, month after month. Be like Joseph. Maintain your chastity and virtue, even though temptation is calling you to yield over and over again.

What was beautiful about Joseph was the glory of God in his life. When we see the theme of beauty in the scripture it is often related to an unusual grace on the person's life, the anointing of the Holy Spirit. If the bible highlights someone's beauty there is a reason. Their beauty is connected to a mission or destiny on their life. Every man and woman should be as beautiful as Joseph if the Glory of God is resting on their lives. You are beautiful in Jesus Christ. You are beautiful when you are walking in the Spirit of God. It does not matter what your physical appearance is, when there is radiance upon your personality because it has been sanctified by the Holy Spirit—that makes you a beautiful person.

In this story, God is telling the brothers to maintain their virtue and to let that speak for them. 1 Chronicles 16:29 shows a connection between the beauty of Joseph and the beauty of God: "Worship God in the beauty of holiness." If holiness is a thing we raise up to we will see the beauty of it. We will see the glory of it. There is a beauty upon Joseph's life because he is a holy man and living according to the will of God. But his reverence for God was the motivation to this holiness that was manifested in his life. Joseph's holiness and righteousness for God motivated him to live by getting proper rest, maintaining a healthy diet, by making the most honorable decisions, and maintaining his devotion to God. It wasn't a matter of Joseph simply looking to God, but a matter of Joseph living well. It was his relationship with God that made him think before he acted, so he thought out his decisions and what ramifications these decisions had on his relationship with God.

The Scripture is trying to tell us Joseph was a man of integrity and his righteousness and faith were integrated with his lifestyle. He lived in a way where he was a whole person. One day the church will get the message that a part of your worship is to eat right. Part of your worship is to get proper rest. Part of your worship is to make godly decisions on a daily basis. Part of your worship is to keep your bible study and your prayer time sacred before God. That was important in Joseph's life and is why Joseph was as beautiful as he was, because he had a holistic approach to life and was a very healthy person.

Joseph lived according to this word that Paul used in Ephesians 5:15 called "a circumspect life." Morning Star's covenant tells us to "walk circumspectly in the world, be just in our dealings, faithful in our engagements and exemplary in our deportments." But what is that? What does that mean? It means to redeem the time and buy up every opportunity to do what is right in the sight of God. It has to do with living an accurate life. It has to do with making sound decisions and having sound judgment. Be where you are going to be when you say you are going to be there. Do what you say you are going to do when you say you are going to do it. Don't offer to engage in things that are not of God just because you want to acquiesce to what your friends and family are acquiescing to.

Virtue and chastity are important. To make it clear, adultery is having sex when you are married to someone else. Or when someone else is married and you are having sex with him or her. Fornication is having sex not in the covenant of marriage. These are wrong in the sight of God and they are not being preached on enough. We are called to be chaste. 1 Thessalonians 4 says we should abound more and more about how we walk and how we should please God…abstain from sexual immorality and know how to live as God has called us. We should encourage that a man or woman ought to live and keep their bodies for Jesus Christ. Do not allow the pressures of this world to tell you it is alright to use and abuse your body anyway you want to because everyone else is doing it. That is not the word of God nor how you ought to live.

The Bible requires us to bring this temple under subjection that we might live transparently before God and maintain our chastity the best we can. If you are a virgin, so what if no one else is, hold on to your holy living like Joseph. If you are not married, go back to abstaining from sexual activity so you will live longer. God will give you prosperity for it and you will add years to your lives. There are many scriptures on it. When you watch men and women succeed and excel in promotion by God, being mightily used by God for years or decades and great grace is upon their lives, watch how they honor this vessel. It is in a way that pleases God. And if you see great people who are mightily gifted, but not mightily used by God, watch how they keep this vessel. They don't maintain this vessel.

Some men have married multiple times but whenever a man leaves the wife of his youth, he also leaves the promises of God's blessing that are upon his life. You find a man in ministry, once he leaves the wife of his youth, also breaks the covenant relationship that had brought him to where he was in ministry. And his ministry is never the same. This is really connected to the covenant relationship. The way you keep your body is really connected to the covenant relationship with God. Joseph said [to Potiphar's wife], "This man has put everything before me, only keeping you. Why do you want me to sin *against God?*" He understood that the way he maintained his body had to do with his relationship with God. Whether you accept it, know it or like it, holiness is still the standard for the Lord. Joseph was called to maintain holiness and it got him in trouble.

In verses 8 and 9 of Genesis 39, Joseph was saying "your husband has giving me a trust that I consider sacred." When you violate a sacred trust the whole world comes down. You cannot violate a sacred trust. When you violate a sacred trust the foundation is destroyed. You cannot do it. You cannot violate a sacred trust. People do it all the time and those who are hurt never recover. Joseph was saying, "You may be beautiful in all but that is not the issue. The issue is that your husband trusts his household to me and I cannot violate that." This idea of "sacred trust" runs all through scripture. If someone entrusts you with great responsibility or sensitive information, to dishonor is to violate the code of life and relationship. If someone has trusted you with their heart, with their property, their children, or with their secrets, consider that sacred, a sacred trust; and do not violate it, even if it leads to your own hurt. If someone came to you in the name of Jesus Christ and gave you a secret, don't violate that trust. If they have trusted you with something that is vital to their well-being and they shared it with you, don't violate it. The whole world comes down on them and you when you violate it. The moment you recognize that is what you have, then you serve with all diligence to uphold that sacred trust.

Because Potiphar has committed everything to Joseph, Joseph was more diligent to maintain everything in his household to make sure that everything was taken care of. What has God entrusted you with? Have you acknowledged, having been given a sacred trust that you must serve with all diligence to make sure that what God has entrusted you with, you will bring it back with interest? What have you done with the gift that God has trusted in your care? A lot of people in the house of God join 14 auxiliaries, but everyone can't sing in the choir, serve on the usher board, etc. There are many things creatively that we ought to discover in the house of God.

Wouldn't you hate to find out the Lord sent you to your church to help your pastor carry out a vision and you never did it? You just enjoyed the word. You never took the gift God entrusted you with to do something. Paul was exalted as a Pharisee, but he met Jesus on the Damascus Road and ran to serve God most diligently because he felt that Jesus had entrusted him with the Gospel and he held that as a sacred trust and ran for his life. In 1 Timothy 1:12, Paul says he has been entrusted and powered by God to carry out this ministry that he was not worthy of, and he does it with all his heart and soul because the Lord has shown this kind of mercy to him in his life. 2 Timothy 1:8-10 supports this. Paul says because "the Lord has entrusted me with the Gospel to the gentiles, I am in prison now. By his mercy he took me from being a persecutor and made me an apostle and because of this, I am in prison. And I run." 1 Timothy 6:17, Paul says God entrusts people who are rich with wealth to serve the body of Christ. But the point is this: Paul is saying "Guard what is in your trust." What has been entrusted to you, hold as sacred and protect it with your heart. When you look at the ministry of Jesus, you see God the father entrusting Jesus with the salvation of the world. Because of the sacred trust that the Father gave to the Son we are here today.

Joseph wasn't just working for Potiphar. Joseph realized that God had given him a sacred trust by being over all that Potiphar had and Joseph would not violate it by laying with Potiphar's wife. He was home alone with her, faithful, because his master and friend had put everything in his trust. Trust is not worrying about the things that I gave you even though I am not around to see you. I'm not going to worry about what you are going to do with my children, property, secrets, or heart because I have entrusted you with it. In John 5 Jesus says, "I do nothing of myself" because "the Father has committed and [trusted] all judgment to the Son, so that all should honor the Son, just as they honor the Father..." Joseph said to himself, "Because he trusted me with this, I will do nothing against him." In the Book of Revelation, the elders praise and worship God and the Son. God shares his glory with no one but the Son. Jesus gives his life because God has given him a sacred trust. Pastors have a sacred trust. Spouses have a sacred trust. Being a parent or friend is a sacred trust. Having a job is a sacred trust. If you violate the sacred trust the whole world comes down.

Chapter 6
THE SACRED TRUST
PART II

The early church, which led revival, was a group of about 200 people. Revival was that every night people responded to the move of God. Revival is every day not only Sunday morning.

Genesis 39:10-19

Joseph was a young beautiful man, in appearance and spirit, and Potiphar's wife came after Joseph. But he refused because he was accountable to God and to his master Potiphar.

What do you do when your integrity gets you into trouble? How do you live through slander?

Our world is not one of straight lines. It is a world of chaos pointing to order and a mystery searching for truth. It's a place where fairness is almost invisible and is sacrificed on a daily basis. The pure in heart are victims of the mighty and the powerful. Christianity as a religion does not make sense. We embrace the symbol of the cross, something that is a sign of capital punishment. It doesn't make sense that God's son, co-creator of the universe, would walk among us and then we call him a liar and crucify him. What really killed Jesus Christ was slander. That's what kills a ministry, a minister, a young woman or man's virtue, honesty and trust. Potiphar's wife slandered Joseph and he was sent to jail.

When Jesus Christ comes back he will judge fairly because he can read the heart. The world is out of balance and when we try to live for Christ we feel pressure but we bring the moral universe into balance. The intent to do right now helps put things in balance. A person who tries to live for God is a threat to compromise because the world lives off compromise. As a consequence they become a threat to the status quo. Evil people try to attack you and while they are doing so God is listening. He doesn't have to do anything about it because he is doing deeper, more mysterious work. He is choosing to build our faith instead of our maneuverability to move around storms. We live in a tension between good and evil. Get used to the tension of a dynamic spirituality and the tension that will come with it.

The main reason why we are to be virtuous all the time is because of the Christ in us. The reason why the virtue will get us in trouble is the Light in us. Light offends and hurts darkness; darkness cannot comprehend the light and attacks it [John 1: 4, 5]. Darkness finds unrest in the light. People are not comfortable around you when you are trying to do the right thing. The more spiritual you become, the more righteous you become, the more humble you will become as you become aware of your sinful nature. As you become more sensitive to the Holy Spirit you also become sensitive to other things, like sin. Light does not contend. Light does not fight back. Light shines. Light does not have to prove anything. Light simply shines. If you get rejected for your witness, your witness will speak for itself. You do not have to justify yourself. When you are seeking God and trying to live for the Lord the first thing Satan will come after is your reputation [Isaiah 54:6].

Fighting spiritual warfare makes you tired. What you do to maintain your witness will exhaust you. That's why Paul says, "Be not weary in well doings, because if you hold on you will reap if you do not faint." [Galatians 6:9] If you get tired you will make the wrong decisions, you will begin to doubt God, you will try to feed yourself things that are not good for you. All the things that Joseph went through made him tired.

What do you do when you have to live with slander, and more of the people who care about it, believe it than believe you? You have to remain faithful to the truth. The only way the world can reject the light that's in the bottle is to destroy the bottle. Joe Wilson can't go after President Obama on the content of his policy, so he attacks his character. He calls him a liar. Whenever your name is slandered someone else will always know the truth, even if the town puts a red letter on your chest. You can count on your friends when you have been slandered, they will come to your aid and your rescue while the others run.

In 2 Timothy 1:16 when Paul went to jail, some of his contemporaries said God was not with him anymore which was why he was in jail, but Onesiphorus came every day to support him and that was a refreshing for Paul. Proverbs 12:9 says, "Better to be persecuted and have one person stand by your side, than to uphold your name by yourself." The only way the enemy can hinder you is slander, which is how Satan attacked Jesus. We often have to acquiesce to slander even though we are right because the pressure of evil is so great. No matter how honest Joseph was he still incarcerated. Someone in the house had to know

Potiphar's wife was sexually reckless. Surely she tried to seduce some young man before Joseph. Yet no one stood up for him.

In Psalm 69:1-4, it says there are times in your life when you have to pay back what you did not steal. Those who are not of God don't pay it back, that is a sign. Those who are of God will take the lower road if it is going to bring peace. Slander will produce some of the best prayers you will ever pray. When you are going through slander you have no choice but to hunker down. If you have to cut yourself off or isolate yourself to keep your sanity, do so. The prison was a safe place for Joseph. In time, the room that God will let you into will be wider than the room that you came into before you were slandered. When you hunker down who knows when to come out because the criticism will always be there. But when you look up one day the anointing and grace of God will have you in a wider place than you were before. You'll look around and say "my soul looks back in wonder." Jesus dealt with slander his entire ministry—you want the anointing, then you can expect slander.

In Matthew 12:22-24, Jesus heals a man who was deaf and blind and the religious leaders said he did it by the power of Satan. That followed Jesus his entire ministry. It never left the mind of the Scribes and Pharisees. When you come back into the wide room not everyone is going to believe you. You live the Christian life and grow through the power of subtraction. You slough off people. Not everyone is going to receive you back into his or her social circles but when you look around the room it is going to be wider.

Chapter 7
THE SACRED SPACE
OF PRISON

There are two types of people in the world: The ones who allow their circumstances to transform their lives and the ones who allow their lives to transform their circumstances. The Holy Spirit is walking with God day by day and allowing the ordinary things of life to speak to you about God.

Genesis 39: 19-21

Potiphar could have killed Joseph, he was in his right, but possibly Potiphar had recognized the grace over Joseph and his spirit, and he knew his wife. To save face before his wife and the people, he put him in prison and spared his life. He put him in the jail that was under his charge because he did not want to depart from the grace that was from Joseph. He made sure he could bring Joseph close enough to him he could still be bathed by the radiance of the grace of God that was on his life. The chief officer over the jail turned over all the business of the jail into Joseph's hand. All of us in some way will experience some type of confinement. We will be in a situation we can't get out of for a while. What do we do? Do we cry, "Woe is me" and blame God? Or do we trust God in the confinement and look for opportunities for redemption? The circumstances of our lives are a background to our relationship with God. God writes the narrative in our lives in a way we wouldn't write it and then reveals in us grace and strength we didn't know we had and a testimony that proves that our faith is enduring. To be truly Christian is to live beyond the risk of your safety. You cannot reach anyone for the Lord by being afraid. If you want to be effective for the Lord Jesus Christ in a world of violence then you must come to a point that the testimony of redemption is upon you.

The prison system represents punitive control by those in power over those who challenge their power. The prison system is ignorant of the difference between those who are righteous or wicked. See Matthew 27 for example. Every now and then God will send someone to overhaul a people. We have a church system that is in need of overhaul. Our system is predicated on numbers and culture, theology instead of biblical truth. We in America preach prosperity but how can we take that message to other nations? Joseph was in prison because he would not compromise his integrity. If he did the prison he would be bound in would be worse because he would be guilty in his own heart. The Lord has often used people in personal confinement in awesome ways. If your faith ever brings you to your limit and you finally cross it you will bless the world and will bring change—you won't have to attempt to do it, God will do it through you.

Bunyan's *Pilgrims Progress*, King's Birmingham speech, Paul's Epistles, the Revelation of Jesus Christ to John…are all prime examples of this.

This message is for someone who feels the laws of this land are against them, they are in such confinement there is nothing they can do. Still, God is there. When we determine our life is not our own we no longer live in shame. Remember, circumstances are only a background for your relationship with God. God often uses prisons as a place to perform miracles, as in Acts 12:5-9. Although Peter was in prison he was sleeping because he had determined he would die for the Lord. Instead of crying, he rested while he was there. Right in the middle of his darkness and incarceration light did shine. When you hit the bottom, being a child of God, light will shine in that situation. Prison walls, barbed wire fences, guards on windows and doors cannot block your fellowship with Jesus Christ; they cannot stop the work of the Holy Spirit and cannot stop your witness to others.

There comes a point in time where the grace doesn't leave, it's in the DNA. Your character can't change because your relationship is in your character. Jeremiah 18:18, (I am paraphrasing) "Let's devise plans to stop Jeremiah because we have discovered that when a man or woman is in a substantive and meaningful relationship with God, we can't stop the relationship." We can't stop the priest from being a priest if he's called. We can't stop the wise from being wise. In Jeremiah 37:11-17, Jeremiah is put in jail but he is still a prophet and when the King needs a word he still has to go down to the jail. In Jeremiah 38:1-6, they put the prophet of God in a pit of mud and excrement where there was no water and he would sink down to eventually die in a matter of moments—still he is in God's will. Your situations and circumstances are only a background to your relationship with God. In Jeremiah 37:10-13 we learn some ministries don't end in a blaze of glory, some end in prison. Before you knew Jesus Christ as Lord and Savior you were in the pit covered with the muck and mire of sin and inequity on your way to die and go to hell. But God sent the salvation in the form of ropes and pulled us out to restoration.

Chapter 8
THE PROBLEM WITH TIMING

Genesis 40

In the OT there are discussions of natural time, prophetic time, and salvific time. In the Greek language, there is *Chronos* time and *Kairos* time. The second relates specifically to divine time. Chronos is quantitative time; Kairos is opportune time. Chronos has to do with the linear understanding of time in terms of time and space. Kairos has the idea of story, order, sequence of events, and their relative meaning to God. As believers, we must understand that we live in both. We will live and become deceased. But we also have a sense of destiny and eternity. Chronos runs away from you and there is never enough time to get all the things done you would like to get done. It is looking at the hourglass. Kairos waits for you, is waiting on you. It is God pushing the button to execute certain events in your life to lead to your destiny. We are constantly frustrated with this. Some of us are waiting for God to push the button so the very things we have been praying about, struggling about, explode. The longer is the wait, the larger is the explosion.

Joseph's story shows the battle between chronos and kairos. It is sad and frustrating—Joseph has to live through the chronos of being falsely accused over and over, put in jail, and forgotten in order for the plans of God for the future. The butler and the chief baker had dreams the same night. Their stories were about chronos—in three days something was going to happen. But kairos took over to explain the destiny and future of these men. Underlying in these stories is the theme of God vindicating the righteous and judging the sins of the wicked. Both men would be affected by their dreams (kairos) in three days (chronos). The three days point to Jonah in the belly of the big fish and Jesus in the grave. We read the scripture and think Joseph is superhuman; never complaining, always praising and ministering, even while in prison.

But in 40:14, 15 we see Joseph's humanity, "Remember me when things start going your way and show me kindness. Talk to Pharaoh about me and get me out of here." I'm so tired of being here, I'm frustrated with this understanding of time (chronos). To believe in God is to believe in divine timing. This passage starts with "And it came to pass" i.e. a whole lot of time passed and you don't know what God was doing. Or long after your worries caused you to feel forgotten in your situation kairos came to pass. It is a vague phrase and yet very specific, announcing that something is getting ready to happen. The problem with timing is that God's timing is not in agreement with our time. Our frustrations will not make God move any faster. When dealing with God, you have to understand that for most of your life things will not happen the way you want or think they will happen. People will even pass you, walking by with seemingly your blessing in their hand. But if you are not frustrated at some point in your life with the dealings of God, then you are not concerned with the dealings of God. Whatever dreams or desires you had that you walked away from after time passed were not good or big enough for your faith.

In this tension between waiting on God and feeling like God has forgotten you, for every Joseph reading this, there will come a time in your life where you will feel that God has forgotten you and you will lose sight of who you are in Jesus Christ—and there is nothing you can do about it.

Joseph is in prison and Pharaoh's birthday arrives (kairos), and the butler is restored and so busy celebrating he forgets Joseph. Have you ever felt like God has forgotten you? That the best part of your life passed you by? That God's rhema word has left you? That you are too old, too tired, not smart enough, and not innocent enough to walk in that plan? Did you ever feel that perfect job, that perfect man or that perfect woman was back there, some time ago? If what you are looking for in life comes to you too soon, it will be a disaster. You will not be mature enough to sustain it. Thank God for his wisdom and caring enough about you to tolerate you through your frustrations. Eating fruit that's not ripe will make your stomach hurt. You are standing under the tree trying to reach a piece of fruit in your life—but when it is God's timing, the fruit will fall.

The ultimate and primary root in your life is God's specific plan for you. If God didn't arrange the experiences in your life this way you would not have the spiritual underpinnings to create the personality and the radiant spirituality you have. Remember that one day is like a thousand years with God (2 Peter 3:8)!

Job 14:7-9: "If you cut the tree down and the roots of the tree die in the ground, at the scent of water it will start to grow again!" (Paraphrase mine).

In Ezekiel 37 we read about an army bleached dry, nothing but a memory. But at the word of God, and army and nation is resurrected.

GOD IS NEVER LATE!

What do you do if you are frustrated and feel that God has forgotten about you, grace is gone, and your best moment has passed you by? What do you do when you get tired of waiting? What should you do? How should you live? Romans 4:14 states exercise your faith while you're waiting on God, Paul declares in 1 Thessalonians 5:24 "He who calls you is faithful, who will also do it."

Chapter 9
WHEN YOU ARE THE KEY TO MANY ANSWERS

Genesis 41:1-16 (focus on verse 1)

The one thing you must remember about spiritual gifts activated by the Holy Spirit they correspond with crucial needs and work in strategic times. It is not a matter of you using them all the time, or operating when it is convenient. The Spirit's power emerges within you at very critical times. Remember this grace abides in a life yielded to God's use and control. He gives you the gift and then says, "Wait." He sets the stage for your gift to be used. There are times in life when certain stars will shine brighter than others at certain times. It's okay for God to bless others around you because it's not quite your time.

Verse 1 says two full years passed by, (probably the time since the butler's liberation), and Joseph is still in prison. There was no word from God, no special anointing on his prayers, no commendation from the captain of the guard. Maybe he begins to lose hope. Maybe God is not listening anymore. Maybe God has moved on. Maybe after all the trials that he's been through God is now gone. What did Joseph do for two years? What happened to him? Joseph practiced patiently waiting and trusting the Lord. He determined not to get discouraged. The key to the spiritual life is how the individual who trusts in God handles their circumstances in a godly, salvific way. Others are watching how you trust in God and whether or not your faith is strong enough to offer remedy when life is unjust and God stops speaking. When you move from complete discouragement to being ready for your promotion six things happen to you inwardly, as they happened to Joseph.

Frustration (Genesis 40:14, 15). When you start to suffer from "spiritual claustrophobia" the world you are living in is closing in on you. You die from lack of air (hope). You hate your life and you are angry with God.

Disappointment. The time passes and you thought things ought to have changed. "Things should have been better by now." "I should be in a better position in my life right now." You find less strength to speak affirmations as your praise. You think all the windows for your blessings have passed you by, they are now behind you.

Disillusionment. You lose hope and begin to see your life as a failure. You have all these hopes around you and you look at yourself and think you are a failure. That your life is not redeemable at all. At this stage all the vices of Satan become enticing. You think you have nothing to live for so why not go down a self-destructive path.

Resignation. Getting to the point where you say, "I don't know what God is doing. I don't know what is going to happen next. I don't know where I'm headed and it doesn't matter to me any longer. If I stay in this situation or if I get out, so be it. I don't understand what God is doing and it doesn't matter."

Openness. You come to the point where you begin to learn new lessons. It is when you come to the place where it doesn't matter what God is doing that something different sprouts within you. You have abandoned who you thought you would be but you are open to the fact that you are going to be someone else, do something else. You see that God is alive, that He is real. You have new prayers. You are not complaining about your situation, not because your situation has changed, but because you have learned how to conduct yourself in your situation. You don't have to tell people because they can see the change in you. You start to see with new eyes that God could be doing something different in you that you did not see before and did not expect. This stage leads to your meeting with Pharaoh, to your exultation!

Exultation.

All this happens when there is no word from God. When He is not speaking and not saying anything. When there is not fruit on the tree the roots are getting stronger. God doesn't have to do everything on the surface when he is doing something in your life. He may be doing something underneath.

Psalm 105:15-19 says the Lord tested Joseph. The spiritual life has no shortcuts. Any person that becomes a tool of God will go through this same cycle. There will be dark days ahead. You will have to work through disappointment, frustrations, even questioning that God exists. Do not neglect the ministry of patience.

James 1: 4 says, "Perseverance must finish its work so that you may be mature and complete, lacking nothing." Don't try to get out of anything prematurely so you can be well developed. One thing difficult about faith is that God placed in all of us the nature of self-preservation and then told us that we have to die to ourselves! I have, simultaneously, the natural instinct to protect myself and the call to crucify myself. If you get tested too soon, you won't be ready and will have to repeat it all over again. Patience has a ministry. If the Lord called you to something, he called you to wait.

It will come to pass when you finally meet your hour of destiny. Remember when Jesus said to his mother, "Dear woman, why do you involve me? My time has not yet come." [John 2:4] When God brings you to this stage and you finally abandon your own hopes, when you have resigned to be used for someone else's need, destiny will come running your way. The Pharaoh had two dreams and God was doing something. None of his wise men could give him an answer but the answer was in prison. There will be a time in your life when you are mad that God is not using you and your blessings are given to someone else. Your prayer life is almost gone, there's no fire in your prayers, no hope in your heart, and you think God is not using you—it is at that moment when you will have to meet the need of someone else. "But what about me?" You must wait. A time will come when only you will be able to be the answer and to meet the need. That is why you have to know why you are here and what your purpose is. Because when that moment comes and you need to meet the need, you won't know why. That is why Joseph had to sit alone in the jail for two more years. God takes your frustrations and on this side is shaping the situation you will be used for. God strips you before he transports you to your destiny. If the Lord promotes you before your time, you get the glory. But when there is no glory left because there is no hope left, then He uses you because He will get the glory.

Here we see the similarities between the life of Joseph and the life of Daniel. Darius had a dream that no one in the kingdom could answer but Daniel. Times like these require us to know our gifts and purpose. Joseph knew his calling. God was using him to spare a nation by sparing a family. A door opens and closes on a hinge. Some people are hinges in the sight of God. When Jesus was born, Simeon recognized him and went to worship. Eighty years in the making, Simeon was just a hinge. Everyone wants to be David but no one wants to be Jonathan. Everyone wants to be Paul yet no one wants to be Barnabas. Everyone wants to be apostles, but no one wants to be the donkey that Jesus rode on.

God had given Joseph the gift of administration. Everywhere he went he put things in order. He was meant to be prime minister. The movie *Matrix Reloaded* depended on the key maker and some of us will be the key maker. We will be the key that others need to reach certain things and get to certain places. Joseph went from despair in prison to being second in command next to Pharaoh. You don't need to be jealous of anyone because when your moment comes God will give you everything you need and more than you can handle. You are God's instruments and servant. The trials and tribulations are school to prepare you for your moment. God will break you completely by letting the trials be so severe because He loves you so much. There is one thing God has called you to do that no one else can do. When God raises you up don't hesitate to go in that door to use your expertise and knowledge. Do what providence requires. Use your gifts to the glory of God and pray that you will not be bitter because you had to wait so long.

Chapter 10
ARE YOU READY FOR YOUR DESTINY?

Genesis 41:25-49 emphasis 33, 37-49, focus on 47-49

Power is a temptation to us all. People who are poor want money and people who have money want power. Even when children are playing together someone in the group will seize power. People who are not ready to handle power, fame, and fortune often desire power, fame, and fortune. It may be God's will for you to have it but if you acquire it too early you will frustrate the plans of God and the maturation of your ability to handle it. In the church most pastors are leery of people who want to be too close because there is sometimes an underlying agenda that is not always the Holy Spirit. They may be looking for power. Don't seek power, greatness, fame, or fortune, but let it come to you as it is God's will and God's time. Your gifts will make room for themselves. The things the Lord wants you to do and the things you want will come to pass in your life, in its time. I have never found a person be successful, who pursues just power, or a relationship work, when one person pursues just power.

Here Joseph is standing before Pharaoh in all his leadership after being taken from the dungeon and in one day Pharaoh makes him ruler over all of Egypt. All of a sudden, in a moment, in an afternoon even, his aristocracy changes. Does this relate to us? No one comes into promotion or gains their destiny overnight. It happens through a series of events. When Joseph finally arrives to his moment, he can handle it because of what he has gone through. When we finally get to this place of destiny that God has situated for us, after all the prayer, disappointment, failure, and hurt, we are not so impressed by it anymore. It becomes about the work. If you are in a place of great resources and recognition and are surprised you are there, then you don't belong there. If you haven't seen yourself in that place before, then you stumbled upon it—and God might not be in that. You should have seen it first. Remember, any responsibility and leadership given to you is about the work.

There is no doubt Joseph's promotion is of the Spirit of God. But the Spirit also developed him and prepared him for this moment he now stands in. Pharaoh had all the riches of Egypt along with the throne but he did not have the grace of God on his life. You can have a profound impact on people when the grace of God is on your life. Anyone can influence another person, it doesn't matter what position or status in life, but it is moving at the opportunities God gives. As a *slave* Joseph could speak to Pharaoh. Pharaoh had the kingdom but he did not have the wisdom (vs. 38). Sometimes the lesser is more important than the greater.

In 2 Kings 5:1-4 we have a slave woman, no name, sweeping the floor with the answer for mighty Naaman in her spirit. She spoke into his life and changed it. It's recognizing who you are and the opportunities of God. We as children of God should always speak in wisdom. Joseph proved that his gifts were in wisdom and administration. Usually the advisors of kings were priests and spiritual advisors. Joseph did not come from the priesthood but he had the Spirit of God in him. God was showing that He was God over Egypt as well, even though they worshiped idols. God imposed Himself into this land of idolatry. This is where we live, in the US, with all these small gods.

Notice that Joseph's dream never told him this. He saw only himself greater in his own family and never as great as the leader of Egypt. Why didn't God show him over thousands of stalks instead of twelve? It's because God will not always tell us the extent and reach of our gifts and callings. Sometimes it is never really known. If you will let God use you, God will take you further than you have ever dreamed. When Joseph is raised up there is no family with him. Sometimes your teacher or mentor is invisible. God is pouring into your life. No one arrives into his or her destiny without training and sometimes the training is providence. Joseph arrived at this moment prepared. His training occurred in the pit years before. Don't shun the solitude of confinement when all you have is God. Notice you haven't become bitter. When you've surrendered to God you have to leave friends behind. You come to church to find family but it's hard to find friends. We need one another and cannot make it in this world without one another. The idea of building friendships and relationships is a Christian mandate: "Build yourselves up in the most holy faith." [Jude 1:20]. There will come a time in your life when the only support that matters is the support of God. What do you do when all your mentors die? You become one.

Look at the symbols in Joseph's promotion.

There's a declaration by the Pharaoh. When you arrive at your destiny someone has to declare it. Jesus is the Messiah from birth, but his ministry does not begin until God says, "This is my beloved Son, in whom I am well pleased." [Matthew 3:17]

Pharaoh gives him the signet ring: law and authority (parallels Prodigal Son).

He is given new garments. He gets a new set of garments to express his royalty and change in class from slave to aristocracy. Colossians tells us to wear new garments: clothed in humility, righteousness and holiness.

He receives a gold necklace and chariot behind the Pharaoh. It shows new rank and power.

He is given a new name: Revealer of secrets.

He gives him an Egyptian wife and a wife of the High Priest. It is a sign of high status and citizenship. She births Ephraim and Manasseh.

God's servants should be known by their gifting and not their titles. Once you are known by your gifting you are a server and called upon by your gift. Every gifted person is needed.

How do you know you are ready for promotion?

When the circumstance forfeits itself to your authority.

When Rosa Parks sat down on the bus in Birmingham she caused a ruckus in the status quo, and the preachers came together to meet. MLK Jr., was a young man who had just finished Boston University, and there was no man better equipped to handle the situation, as the other ministers were afraid to try.

2 Samuel 2:1-4. Saul died and circumstance led to the promotion of David. Sometimes you have to wait for the other generation to pass on. The church should not die with the pastor; others should be raised up to continue the ministry.

When your values govern your lifestyle.

People of authority usually have consistent values they were raised with. Whenever you go to a significant place take your values and training with you. The deals are made when a man or woman can look in your face and believe you or believe in you. If you ever find yourself in a place of great significance, what will keep you there are the values you live by.

Your teaching and training will keep you in your destiny.

When you are awed by God's grace but not awed by the circumstances or the people around you.

If Joseph were afraid of Pharaoh he could not have spoken to him.

When others will have to validate your life, gifts, and calling.

See verses 37 and 38.

When something inside of you tells you that you are ready to make a difference. If you are not sure you are not ready.

You know in your heart you can make a difference.

In vs. 47 Joseph worked very hard for seven years. Joseph had a plan and he worked it.

When God gives you a vision.

God gave Joseph a vision. God had a plan and Joseph *followed* God's plan.

The reason so many of us procrastinate is because we don't have a plan.

May we not be afraid to be great and to accomplish great things.

Chapter 11
WE ALL MUST GIVE AN ACCOUNT

Genesis 42:1-24

Joseph is governor and his brothers do not recognize him. He hears them talking as they say, "If we had treated Joseph fairly then this would not have happened to us." About ten years have passed and they are still victims to what they did to Joseph. It could be that some famines we face in life are our fault. Sin causes us to lose spiritual sensitivity. We should be as discerning as anyone else God uses or speaks to, but sometimes our sin takes away our ability to discern. Our hearts are dulled and our energy is given to the livelihood of our sin. It desensitizes us to the work of the Spirit of God.

Joseph had a vision there would be seven years of famine and seven years of plenty. None of his brothers did. They did not discern what was going to happen because they were bound by the sin they committed against Joseph. During the seven years of plenty they did not sense what God was doing and they did not prepare for the famine. They could not discern because they did not confess and they did not repent. You cannot understand the Scriptures as you ought to as long as your sin is not confessed. Discernment will return when the sin is confessed and time has passed to bring healing. Our sins are forgiven before we commit them. We are saved from the beginning of the world, but there is a process of restoration and we are not released from that. The son called prodigal takes his goods, lives a worldly life, and then comes back and says to his father, "I am ready to be your servant." He understands there is a process he must go through to regain his father's trust again. There is a process of restoration. You must reconcile things on earth before you meet God in Heaven. You will give an account for your life and for the lessons you must learn as Christians.

People who come to the Lord still face life's challenges: face court cases, loans, debts, unexpected children, etc. When they come to Jesus Christ past errors surface which must be reconciled so they can go forward to the Lord with a clear conscious. God loves you so much He will force you to deal with the things you buried so when you go to the next level in the Spirit you do not have to spend energy trying to hide the past. We must trust God with our future as well as our past. Joseph's brothers suffered for what they did in their past. First, they suffer famine. Because they were not in the Spirit they did not see the famine coming and they did not save food in preparation. Second, they suffer cruelty from this Egyptian leader. Third, they suffer three days in prison. Here we see fulfillment of Joseph's dream and a reversal of what happened to Joseph. He met his brothers in Dotham, now they meet him in Egypt. They made a decision over his life, now he is making a decision over theirs. Remember we our covered by the blood no matter what happens. His brothers showed him cruelty and had power over him, now he is showing them cruelty and has power over them.

The brothers thought they had buried Joseph but instead they now sit before him and do not recognize him. These are the brothers from which ten of the twelve tribes were named. Their names are echoed through all eternity but they were not perfect. God uses people who are conscious of their own weakness. When a person becomes sensitive to the Holy Spirit they become sensitive to their own sin. The brothers eventually become the leaders of the tribes of Israel but right now they are dealing with the fact that they have sinned against their brother. The famine in the land forced the brothers to go to Egypt to get grain from the brother they cast away. God will let the circumstances in life and world events bring you to repentance. Joseph is a stranger to his brothers because: 1) they thought he was dead; and 2) he is not the same person he was before. He has been in prison, a slave, falsely accused, forgotten, and exalted. Anyone who has had their hand held by God the Father as they go through the trials of life will not come out the same. God is about putting iron in your feet and steel in your spiritual life. When the enemy comes against you, you can keep your peace because you've had no choice but to.

Have you ever been in a place where you were so worried that you stopped worrying? Paul said, "I've learned how to glory in my tribulations because when I am weak, God is strong." Evil circumstances change you, but they change a child of God for the better. Their hearts become soft and they become more dependent on the Lord. Others keep lists and don't forgive. Children of God say, "All things come together for the good of those who are called by God." When you are living in a period of brokenness you have the ability to see past clothes, education, and spiritual imagery, right to where the person is in God: what they are hiding and what they are going through. Joseph's brothers did not recognize him but Joseph recognized them.

Evil circumstances for a child of God are the avenue for promotion. The only scars that Joseph has are on his memory. He is now rich and powerful and his brothers are hurting. When someone abuses you God takes you further, and unless they have taken it to God, they are still in the same place. But if Joseph is a child of God, and the anointed of the Lord, why is he so cruel to his brothers? Why did he put them in prison? Why did he talk so hard to them?

Unconsciously he is dealing with the fact that he was treated cruelly. God was at work in his unconscious to start the process of their recompense.

It was the role of rulers to be cruel to their despots because it was a sign of power. It was a way to keep others at bay—Joseph was trained this way. Notice the brothers began confessing about their brother when he didn't ask them.

Joseph's cruelty and position of intimidation led the brothers to be honest about their family situation. They began confessing on their own.

It was a way of testing their characters to see if they had any remorse and repentance and to see where they were spiritually. Joseph challenged his brothers because he had to know what was inside of them. Sometimes the Lord has to challenge us to see if we will let go of the things we don't need and hold on to the things that really matter. Hebrews says, "…removing what can be shaken- that is, created things- so that what cannot be shaken may remain." [Hebrews 12:27]

It was a way to extract their contrition and their humiliation for their sins years before.

It was a way to make them confront their sinful past and face the consequences of barbarity to Joseph.

Does God forgive sin? Is it true that every sin will find you out? Does the Bible not say if we confess our sins, we have a faithful God who will forgive us and atone us? If this is true, then do we as his children, having confessed our sins, ever have to deal with the recompense?

We have to give an account. Not for everything, but it is God who decides what we give an account for and how. It is the way of practical sanctification. Here is some reinforcement for practical sanctification:

The Lord loves us too much to allow us to escape with ungodly behavior without correcting it. If you drive fast, cut people off and succeed, you may make it a habit. It may be that God will let you have an accident or get stopped so you learn to correct the behavior; because God knows that if you keep cutting people off, one day you will face the 18-wheeler…

God may not expose our sin but it will be addressed in some form. 2 Samuel 16:5-10. God allowed Shimei to curse King David because he committed adultery with Bathsheba.

When a child of God sins against the Lord, sin and guilt go down to the bone. In Psalm 38:1-3 David says, "even though no one knows what I have done, my sin has aged me and my guilt is in the depths of my soul." An evil person can do harm and walk away. A godly person will walk away with many stripes. An over sense of guilt by Satan is just as dangerous but guilt that leads to repentance is what we seek.

The Lord cannot allow anything in your past to bind you in your future because he wants to use you in a mighty way. He will make sure that certain things in your past will be dealt with so that when he raises you up to use you in the most effective way, Satan cannot grab you by the old chains and bring you down.

It is important for us to know the Lord's workings. We must learn how God deals with his servants because as God uses us we must learn how to divine and interpret things in the Spirit of God. Am I going through this for the Lord or for something that I have done? Jonah realized this while in a raging storm at sea with the lives of many sailors in jeopardy and said, "I know this trouble is because of me, I know this storm came about because of my disobedience." [Jonah 1:12] Certain things happen in the lives of other people because of our disobedience.

We are going to Heaven and God wants us to stop running, hiding, and dodging so we can sleep at night. He wants every part of our life reconciled so he can bless us in the future. When a man or woman is growing in God they confess the small sins before the big things happen. They don't wait to build a long list; whatever it is, they bring it early so they don't have to bury a tragedy.

1 Corinthians 11:27-32

Therefore, whoever eats the bread or drinks the cup of the Lord in an unworthy manner will be guilty of sinning against the body and blood of the Lord. A man ought to examine himself before he eats of the bread and drinks of the cup. For anyone who eats and drinks without recognizing the body of the Lord eats and drinks judgment on himself. That is why many among you are weak and sick, and a number of you have fallen asleep. But if we judged ourselves, we would not come under judgment. When the Lord judges us, we are being disciplined so that we will not be condemned with the world.

God sometimes brings things up again because they weren't dealt with or confessed so we might deal with them and go on with our spiritual life.

Tomorrow is a blessing. *Tomorrow* you will be anointed and used by God. *Tomorrow* prosperity will come. So we must give an account *today*.

There are NO DETOURS in Christ!

Chapter 12
HANDLING GRACE

Most people don't know how to react to blessings because most of us look at our lives like a series of shoestrings tied together. The left shoestring represents the good season and the right shoestring represents the bad season. So one goes through life expecting that with every good season there is going to be a bad season around the corner or underneath. We can't expect grace because we sometimes feel unworthy. We know all the bad things we have done and the poor witness we've been, so why would God want to do anything for us. Joseph's brothers left their brother in the pit and what do they get for it? Bushels of grain! They come with a little money and then go home with their money and more grain than they could afford. The story is now on Joseph's brothers and father because they are about to walk into the purpose of God. Let us compare and contrast the reaction of Joseph's brothers and the action of Joseph toward them. The brothers were confused about the message. Why did Egypt's new ruler show kindness to the sons of Jacob? Why could they secure more grain than they could afford or were worthy of? Was this a trap that Joseph setup to accuse them? Did Joseph know that his act of generosity of giving his brothers grain and their money back would cause them to live in fear?

What do you do and how should you respond when you receive more kindness than you deserve?

Upon discussing these things with the father, Jacob feels like the family is falling apart. Right at the very moment when God is about to preserve Jacob's family and bring them into 400 years of grace and prosperity, he feels like having a funeral. Right before the break though, things appear to be at their worst. In that season praise God because you are about to come into a new destiny and purpose. You are about to find a path of life that you would not have discovered unless you had suffered beforehand.

Joseph gives his brothers what they don't deserve. That is called grace. There are many manifestations of grace.

Grace is receiving goodness when you deserve punishment. There is no reason in the world why God ought to be so good to you but not only that, he is training you, keeping you, and preparing you when he has no reason at all to do so. In 1 Timothy 1:12-15, Paul said "I have no reason to preach this Gospel because I was trying to destroy it. But God enabled me to preach his word."

Grace is the overabundant supply of whatever is needed to overcome any situation. Divine sufficiency is God giving someone the ability to do what he or she could not do naturally. God gives us what's necessary to make it when we need to make it. There will be enough grace in our lives to survive it. Paul says, "Lord, take this thorn in the flesh from me," and God says, "My grace is sufficient." In other words, "why don't you thank me for the grace that allowed you to minister to lost souls through the thorn?" These ten men go to Egypt and come back with more than they deserved. That is what God does in the life of the believer. We get the goodness and benefit of God the Father, through Jesus Christ.

When we get blessed we get nervous and think, "Why is this happening to me?" But every blessing is a sign of our journey. If we learned how to recognize the little things God is doing on a daily basis we would realize how important we are to the Kingdom of God. We will never come into great accomplishments, never be used by the Kingdom of God, never come into great exposure, and never understand what it means to be greatly blessed or greatly used by God, unless we learn to handle grace.

Rick Warren, speaking at Willow Creek Community Church in South Barrington, Illinois, in response to the success of his book ministry, said, "All I do is keep walking through the doors that God opens."[2] He has learned how to handle grace. We will never succeed until we learn how to handle God doing things for us which we do not deserve. Expecting good things to always go your way is pride. Expecting bad things to always go against you is also pride. When you learn to accept things in your life by faith, you are a recipient of faith. When you accept whatever the Lord sends, and see that the Lord is trying to teach you something, that is grace.

Grace is never about the recipient; grace is about the giver. God's nature is to be a blessing and His desire is to find a man or woman He can trust with His Kingdom. We need to learn to handle grace so we can learn God's dealings with us. Verse 24 reveals while Reuben and his brothers were saying, "these events are because we mistreated Joseph," Joseph wept because he was so happy to see them. It was in his heart to love them and reunite with them. It is Jesus Christ's desire to love on us and shower us with grace and mercy. When we give our lives to Jesus we always end up better than we were before. We don't deserve anything that has happened in our lives but it is His grace. *Study the last verses of 1 Timothy 6 until it is in your spirit.*

Problems are often compounded when God is working to change your future. It seems like troubles all come down on the same day. But God is actually setting the stage for your blessings. When all these things come down on you and you experience anxiety that is all right. Just understand that God is working things out for you. Jacob said, "I am bereaved. I might as well die right now. Joseph is gone. Simeon is gone. Now they want to take Benjamin from me." Joseph was not dead, he was Prince of Egypt. Simeon was not dead, and Benjamin was about to meet his brother and have the biggest banquet ever. The whole family was about to walk into abundant blessings. Don't focus on the circumstances because you will misunderstand the circumstances. Don't say to yourself, "I don't deserve the grain," say, "Lord, thank you for what you have done!"

Chapter 13
THE FOLLY OF PROCRASTINATION

Genesis 43:1-10, emphasis on 8, 10

No one likes to confront past mistakes or great challenges, we put things off as long as we can whether it is a challenge or a promise. Joseph's brothers put this matter off as long as they could, until the grain ran out and, by necessity, they had to go back. They left their brother Simeon in prison until they were forced to deal with near starvation when the grain ran out. They need to face the man who treated them firmly, whom they did not know was their brother Joseph. Judah and his father Jacob were arguing about Benjamin going on the trip. Jacob is fearful the same fate Joseph faced will befall Benjamin. Feeling Judah's predicament, I would have said, you can choose not to forgive me and blame me for losing Benjamin and I will live with the rejection from you. Then he says, "For if we had not lingered (procrastinated) we would have dealt with this issue by now and have returned with grain already."

Procrastination is lingering on the edge of fear, failure, and great success in life. Many of us would have been more successful if not for procrastination. The opportunities were there and the settings were right for success but we were too afraid or too lazy and the door closed. At the root, procrastination is pride. If we had depended on the Lord and not ourselves we would not put things off because putting things off equates to saying "this thing is easy" or "I can do this anytime" not realizing that the Lord could close the doors as he chooses. Some of us are serial procrastinators. When we procrastinate it does not mean we don't have the ability to get things done or are not courageous enough to face the challenge, we just choose to address it at a later time. We are not willing to devote the time and effort needed to address the issue for whatever reason and we put it off.

The greatest sin a person can commit is the pursuit of bliss: a painless, problem less, happy-go-lucky existence. For some reason we believe that if the Holy

Spirit is operating in our lives and we are covered in the blood we will live a blissful life. But that is not in the Bible. It is a promise from the enemy. Satan promises us an easy life. Instead of looking for bliss we should be looking for God's will no matter how difficult because it is better to be in the will. Bliss can look like an extra hamburger or a glass of wine or anything that can add to our addictive behavior. Bliss is false at its root and always present in the life of the procrastinator.

What does the Bible say about procrastination?

Proverbs 20:4 (elaborations are mine) When those who have tilled and sown are eating, the lazy person will be begging because it was too uncomfortable and too much work to sow in the winter. Winter is whenever the time is not opportune. Every time someone does something great for God, it is never the right season. Do not look for the perfect opportunity to do something for God, look for the word instead of the right season. The right season says that you are the judge in determining God's will and that your own understanding determines what is best.

Matthew 25:1-12: The foolish had the door closed on them because they procrastinated and did not get oil.

Proverbs 24:10: When a person chooses to give up because they face a task that is difficult. This wall of avoidance comes up because the task is hard. There is no such thing as putting it off for another time.

Proverbs 6:6-11: "I'm tired right now; I need a rest or nap. Oh, now I have a little headache, etc. What's wrong with a little rest?" You'll wake up one day and be in poverty. You will look around one day and you will have nothing. God requires of us **labor**! No one tells us when we give our lives to Christ we have to work, labor, and sow. The ant has not a supervisor but knows there is a season to gather food, a season to store food, and a season to rest.

The Bible is very strong and adamant against procrastination. Procrastination is disobedience. None of us want to be disobedient but to say to God "I will do it later" is disobedience, which is like the sin of witchcraft. If we avoid things that are difficult, we will inevitably shut God out because we are saying, "My way is better than your way." If we learn to respond immediately we will keep from missing God in that way. Judah said if they had dealt with this sooner instead of waiting for the grain to run out, they would not be having this conversation. But they put it off as long as they had grain. This is not to say we should not wait in doing God's will. When God tells Abram his wife is going to have a baby, he has to wait for it. Samuel anoints David and has to wait. Jesus was born anointed as Messiah and has to wait.

Luke 9:57-61: Jesus tells the excited man, "Calm down, you see the glory, but you don't see the sacrifice." Jesus told the other man, "You dealing with your father's sickness is procrastination." James, John, Peter, Andrew immediately dropped their nets and followed Jesus. This scripture shows us the Lord will not accept any excuse, no matter how righteous. We seem to be able to justify everything accept obedience.

Jeremiah 13:15: God has already said to you, "Thus says the Lord." Don't let your pride cause you to be obstinate when God is speaking. Verse 16, God has spoken and you need to do God's will and follow his word before the night comes, while you are still young, astute, and strong. We must do God's will while we have the time, because our salvation is nearer now than it was before. Don't let your pride make you a procrastinator.

Genesis 43:15: The brothers are procrastinating about going to face Joseph and Joseph is getting a banquet ready for them. Here we are putting off God's will and what he's telling us, and he is saying, "Come dine with me. I am about to bring you into deep communion, deep fellowship, great blessings, exceedingly and above all you could ask or think. And you procrastinate because you are afraid I will judge you."

Proverbs 12:24: Leaders work hard and become leaders because they are willing to work harder than others. The hand of the diligent shall rule. The one that will wind up on top will be the one that worked harder, prayed harder, cried more, served more than any other. We must look back over our lives, ask God what we procrastinated about and ask for forgiveness. Then we need to ask God to forgive us for procrastinating about how we hear him. If we are not willing to work hard and obey the Holy Spirit we will end up right where we don't want to be. We have the ability to adjust. We must work hard to do the will and we must not procrastinate when the Spirit of God gives us a way to go forward.

Because the brothers avoided facing Joseph, they avoided the banquet.

Chapter 14
THE BANQUET

Here we see the fulfillment of prophecy and Joseph's dream.

As we think about the story of Joseph think about how he changed and yet remained the same. This is the man who was betrayed by his brothers, falsely accused, left in prison and now exalted over all of Egypt second only to Pharaoh. He must go out and cry because he still loves his brothers so much. Love covers a multitude of sin.

There is still prejudice that we see. Joseph eats by himself because of stature, the Egyptians ate by themselves, and the Hebrews ate by themselves.

Joseph's story is leading to this part, the Banquet. The Banquet is so beautiful because its theological concept is that of salvation. God is introducing us to the Holy Spirit in the OT, the idea of lasting fellowship and communion with the King. The idea of the banquet as the symbol of salvation runs from Genesis to Revelation. They sit down together and eat, feasting and fellowship. Compare to Revelation 20. The NT was inaugurated at a banquet; Jesus sat down with his disciples and had supper. One of the extraordinary moments of scripture is Jesus feeding the multitude with a few fish and a few loaves of bread. The Scribes and Pharisees understood ceremonial washing before eating to be imperative because the fellowship was not only with family, but also with God. We eat in the presence of God who blesses us with enough to break bread with one another. In Exodus 24: 9 and 11, the Israelites are at Mount Sinai. People die approaching this mountain, but the veil is pulled back and they are allowed to get near pure divinity, the very personality of God and they have their food. God is right there, they can almost touch him and they realize they are in the very presence of God and are not dead. And they feast!

This story is all about the banquet. The brothers who are estranged come back into fellowship. When Adam sinned and passed it to us, angels of the Lord blocked off the presence of God with the sword. But one day we will be brought back into the presence. If we cannot have fellowship down here how can we expect to have fellowship with God in Heaven? Jacob tells the sons that when they go bring an offering of atonement, the best that they have to placate the Egyptian ruler. They had some things, but it wasn't enough. Jacob says although this offer may be meager and little, just take what they had and offer it anyway. Our offerings to the Father are not that much but why not take what we have and offer it anyway and see what the Father does?

You are dealing with the misery of your "lost-ness." So you decided to surrender your heart and soul to Jesus Christ because you are tired of being beaten and tortured by your guilt of disobedience. What else do you have to bring? You say you brought your heart, but you didn't bring your heart. You brought a decision. But what else do you have to bring? Unless you bring something else you will not experience atonement. What else do you bring here? You must bring something to the altar: names, acts, habits. You must bring something before you can experience God's power to change your life. Something must be left. You have to placate the King. Good Christian doctrine says that God is our atonement and we only have to bring our heart and soul. Yes, that is true. But if you want to experience the true power of God you must come to the altar with your life, your money, your job and/or your relationships. When you realize they are not yours any longer then God can deal with you about those things.

If you do not bring them then Christ is not allowed to work in those areas which Satan has used against you. When the brothers went before Joseph they brought what they had: some balm, spices, a little bit of myrrh, some honey, some pistachio nuts, and almonds. In Jacob's day, you did not go before anyone with power without bringing something. This is no small matter. This is a gift to bring to someone who has the fate of your life in his or her hands. If there is a man or woman of God in your life you ought to bring something to them. Bring something when you come before the Lord. Each of the fruits represents something of the best quality that they had worldwide. The gifts were the most unique and fertile from the land. They were meager, but special. None of those items were native of Egypt, they were native of Palestine. For example, pistachio nuts were from Northern Galilee.

When they brought those things they reminded Joseph of home. It was the food from home. But what was that food in the comparison to the abundance and vast storehouses of Egypt? They were miniscule, almost nothing. In Genesis 43:16 Joseph told the servant to kill an animal for brothers and give them money. What they brought could not be compared to what they received. God is not caught up on what you bring because whatever you bring cannot be compared to what you will receive from God the Father. God doesn't need our money in Heaven! Genesis 43:23 shows what they got from their little offering. They got their brother, they got money, and they got the family restored. Our offerings cannot be compared to the offerings of the Kingdom but without the offering we cannot have this communion.

Psalm 24:1 says the earth is the Lord's and the fullness thereof, so whatever we give to God we give him his own possessions. Everything we do for the Lord matters. What we give to God in natural things, God gives to us in spiritual blessings. The children of Macedonia gave to Paul over and over again, and Paul tells them they have added to their account in Heaven and that God will supply all their needs according to the riches in Heaven. We offer Christ and God the Father our meager prayers; Romans says we don't even know how to pray properly. But the Holy Spirit transforms our prayers and what does God give us in return? His presence, his power, answers. We give him our tithes and offerings—a few dollars here and there, yet God gives us his Kingdom. We offer God our time—15 minutes here and there—and he gives us a reward: A crown of righteousness that will not fade away. We give a little glass of water and we get an eternal reward. The very thing we thought did not count was waiting before God. What Jacob offered to Joseph was not enough to live on and we can only offer God out of our own resources. We cannot give God someone else's life, time, or resources, we can only give our own. When David went to buy the threshing floor he said, "I couldn't take this freely because I can't give to God what was not mine."

The balm, honey, myrrh, and spices are all symbols of salvation and the Holy Spirit. (Compare balm in Gilead, Jonathan's honey, the three Wise Men's spices and myrrh.) The almonds budded from Aaron's staff. What about the pistachio nuts? They grew freely in Palestine. They gave to Joseph what they had an abundance of and we can give to God what we have an abundance of. We must give to God whatever we have an abundance of, whatever we are rich with. Our relationship with God is more substantive when we make sacrifices. It means more when we make sacrifices. This message is about learning to make sacrifices in faith and letting God have access to every part of us. Our time, our relationships, our resources, our gifts—no matter how meager they may be can be used of God. Never think that you don't have enough to be a blessing to the Kingdom of God, he will take us where we are and take our little and transform it to something great for the Kingdom of God.

1 Chronicles 29:10-14 says "God we give to you only what comes from your hand. For thine is the Kingdom, thine is the power, and thine is the glory."

Chapter 15
THE TEST OF FAITHFULNESS

There is no heavy lifting in Christ: "Take my yoke upon you and learn of me; for I am meek and lowly in heart: and ye shall find rest unto your souls. For my yoke is easy and my burden is light." Matthew 11:29, 30

What if you knew the power of all miracles is faithfulness? That the power of God to move in a situation is someone's faithfulness? That it's not just the person who wants the miracle but someone else being faithful in that individual's life to see miracles happen? In Matthew 15:21, the Canaanite woman came asking Jesus for a miracle and Jesus told her, "your faith in what I can do is great and your faithfulness to your daughter is great; and that will cause the miracle to happen." We will have more miracles in our lives if we are more faithful to the people in our lives. Our family and friends need us, our prayers, faith, love, prayers, etc. and we are instrumental in their deliverance. There is a place in the Spirit where it is not about you but the people who need you.

Genesis 44:1-45:3a

(Verse 5, do you think sometimes God sets people up?)

Judah says, "Okay, the boy took the stuff, but I assured Father that he would come back. Take me instead." His words move Joseph to reveal himself. The Scriptures do not tell us at all when Joseph was going to reveal himself. But at the words of Judah, he could not keep the charade up any longer.

Joseph has four significant interactions with his brothers: 1) when they sell him in to slavery; 2) when they come to buy provisions; 3) when they have the banquet; 4) and this interaction with the cup, plot and a test. Here is the man of God with this devious plot. Why would he do that and why would God allow such a thing? The brothers leave the Egyptian's home with contentment and joy and as soon as they leave the outskirts of Egypt they are under arrest, threatened with death and slavery. You think all is going well but then the hope of your future is taken away. Maybe God is going to do something else. Maybe every storm you go through is intended to take something from you that you can't take to Heaven and God wants to give you something you can't live without. Maybe every storm is to strip us and give us something in its place?

When they arrive at the House of Joseph they immediately fall down prostrate before him—the fulfillment of Joseph's dream. God never breaks his promises. If God puts a rhema word in your spirit and it takes 15 years to come to pass, it will still come to pass if God said it. Remember, Benjamin was the only full brother of Joseph the rest were half-brothers. The test is this: Would the brothers treat Benjamin the same way they treated Joseph years earlier? Whatever God promises you there is no glory or promotion until you are ready. There are no shortcuts. The great servants of God are all made the same way: Shaped on the anvil of time, broken to the point of nothing, they go through a shedding and re-creation. If Joseph's brothers couldn't stand up for Benjamin they did not learn from their mistakes.

Consider verses 5 and 15: The servant and Joseph say this is a cup that helps him see the future. Why did God allow this lie to be used? The cup of divination is the ability to discern events using this instrument. When the High Priest wore the twelve stones to represent the tribes of Israel, the stones would light up at a word from God. This cup is really a reference to tea leaves. The servant was saying, "My master looks in this cup and can tell the future." Joseph agreed as a part of his plot to deceive his brothers. God is saying, "Don't make claims about your spirituality that are not true." It's called hypocrisy and friends and family have an antenna that can read it. Jesus never did that. He asked, "Why do you call me good?" He had no pretense in his spirituality. Be transparent if you want people to hear your testimony. Don't leave out the humanity and the brokenness.

The Bible takes us back to earth. While Joseph is perpetrating this lie, Judah is saying that no, not your divination but God has uncovered our sin: what they did to Joseph a long time ago. You are blessed if God uncovers your sin to you. You are loved if God gives you the opportunity to see from God's eyes your sinfulness. Judah is a testament to what happened to Joseph's brothers since their betrayal. Listen to how they have grown. Instead of making excuses, listen to what they say (verses 16-34). The brothers grew because they came to a place of abandonment. If there is anything in life you can't live without, the Devil can come after it. But when you reach the point where you can live without anything, then the Spirit can move you. Next they came to a place of contrition before the Egyptian. Eleven times Judah used the word servant to reference himself, his father, and brothers. These men who were so high when they sold Joseph are now merely servants. If they were able to walk away from Benjamin they would never have come to their prosperity. But Judah said, "I cannot leave my brother in Egypt." That is the moment when God will take your intercession and change your situation.

Real ministry is faithfulness, not signs and wonders. Remember Satan will perform signs and wonders. It's not about signs and wonders, the laying on of hands to show that God is real. The miracle is in the fact that you won't leave your loved one when it is easy to leave. The miracle is you are free to leave the situation, but you cannot leave your loved one in the situation. You must be willing to take their place. Judah said, "Let this young man go and keep me here instead." That moved Joseph's heart and that moves the heart of God. When you can say "spare my family/friend and put whatever is on them on me," there is the miracle.

We need to be there for our family members and friends. To abandon them in their distress and selfishly praise God without any concern is hypocrisy. We must advocate for them and cry out to God for them.

If God gives you a vision and that vision takes a while to be fulfilled, it will be greater than what you imagined. You shouldn't want your blessings to come immediately or your stormy periods to end too quickly. Jesus told the Scribes and Pharisees they had their reward. God can give you your reward quickly but if you wait for the storm, if you wait for the coal to become a diamond, it will be more valuable. Because Joseph waited for the vision through prison and being forgotten it was greater than what he envisioned.

There is no promotion without devotion. Anyone who wants spiritual growth and to be used by God effectively must remember they come only as they are used on behalf of other people. There is no promotion in the life of the Spirit if you do not know what it means to be devoted to other people. You want to find a church that is growing and healthy and then find a people that feel that their leaders love them. If it's only about the leaders it will grow hot and fast, but then the head will be cut off. Joseph listened to Judah, watched his life, his advocacy for Benjamin, and it moved him so much that he couldn't handle it anymore.

When MLK Jr. spoke, his words emanated with us for one reason: The power of the Holy Spirit was manifested in the tone. When a man or woman has been moved by God it will be revealed in the different use of their words; it's not in the rhetoric, but in the tone. When Joseph heard the tone of Judah's voice, the earnestness of his request and the words he used, it unlocked something. You can tell the difference when someone has all the words and most fall the wrong way, and when someone has few words and they all fall the right way.

Luke 18:9-13 (truth's tone): There are two prayers. Both true. But one had a different truth. There was no power in the Pharisee's prayer. All the power was in the prayer, "Lord have mercy."

We all make mistakes and we all do wrong, but we can fix it quickly if we go to God humbly.

The miracle of the cross is that the Lord Jesus Christ loved us so much that he left Heaven and died on the cross in shame.

Real ministry is not in doctrine, not in methodology, but in faithfulness.

Chapter 16
I AM JOSEPH

2 Peter 1:1: A lot of our mistakes are made because we don't know who we are in God. We are discontent, jealous, and insecure because we don't know who we are and who we should be. But we are growing in the Lord. Life is difficult because there is a destiny on our lives.

Genesis 45:1-3a

"I am Joseph." But who is Joseph really? Joseph is the person who without any choice of their own, the expectations on their life is higher than that of their family members and friends. Thus, they cannot get away with the same things. By nature Joseph just takes on more. He takes on his problems and the problems of those close to him. Joseph waits longer, he suffers more, he gets criticized more, he works harder, and he has an innate burden to be more responsible than others. If this is you it's because God composed your personality as such so that your life will be liberating and affect change in a powerful way. In this scene, Judah is appealing for Benjamin and Joseph could take it no longer and reveals himself. But what happened to me was not your fault God was doing something so I may save the family. I had to endure much hardship to get to this place. Remember, here they thought Joseph was dead and they have had three dealings with this Egyptian before they discover this is their brother.

What is the *Unlikely Blessing*?

Divine providence leading you through problems and adversity to come into divine prosperity and favor. Receiving your divine destiny after you have been tested to your limits. If you want the best of God you must be tested to your limit, brought to your breaking point, and only after will you be able to see what God is doing.

God finally answering the nagging question of your purpose. We spend most of our lives trying to figure out who we are but when we come into our destiny, God pulls it all together and we see who we are and where we are going next.

Joseph is not afraid of being great. He was prepared all his life for greatness. Joseph believes that he is worthy to be used by God.

The ability to replace bitterness and vengeance with loving kindness toward your enemies.

If you are Joseph one day you will come to a place in life where you can see the favor of God.

Joseph is united with his brothers, has experienced reconciliation. Joseph lives for reconciliation and to have broken relationships mended. He has the capacity to reconcile with other people. Reconciliation is the greatest theme of human existence. We should pray for it. In Genesis, when Adam and Eve disobeyed they were no longer able to have communion with God. But Revelation ends in reconciliation: "The tabernacle of God is with man."

2 Corinthians 5:20: "We are all ambassadors of God to the world with responsibility to say "be reconciled with God."

The most powerful and dangerous force we will have to face in the near future is violence. The church is not prepared to face the violence. But with the things that are going to happen with violence in America, the Lord is going to purify the church. Your ability to suffer is going to define your faith. The answer is not simply a restraining order but wisdom from God and prayer, teaching how to disarm violent people in our lives. It's time for the people of God to be strong and nonviolent.

When Joseph revealed his identity, he was saying Egypt changed me but I am still Jacob's son. When he bathed, he bathed in the sweetest incense, received the finest education, etc. The outside may have changed but he was still the same at the core. The *id* remains original. You may react differently to your situations but your core is the same. When you come into salvation you can finally be who you were meant to be in God. When you come to terms with this your new knowledge gives you new authority. Trials, tribulations, and hardships are not meant to break you but to purge you and eliminate the things you cannot take into the Kingdom. God's will is not for us to destroy people and get them out of our lives, the point is this: First, when you grow spiritually you can discern people who are meant for your destruction; and second, you are not hurt when other people let you down because your reliance is on Jesus Christ and God the Father. When you go through suffering your relationship with God becomes steal, your faith is iron, and your love is gold.

Remember, Joseph was never out of God's will. No matter how hard Joseph's life was God was in it.

Psalms 105:16-22 shows that Joseph was forced to have a hard and difficult life, but God's word came to pass. Whatever promise God made is still in affect. His word will come to pass. It may not be how you want it but it will come to pass.

The message behind Joseph's disclosure is at some point the doors you have been banging on will open and your diligence will bring harvest. You must live your future in your present, because your future will become your present. You must prepare yourself for your future now, by making decisions based on your future. You must carry it out now, because it won't be long before you are there. Your life will have more meaning and you will touch more people that you can imagine. Never think you are too old to come into your destiny. Will some people miss the will of God in their lives? Yes, but not you. Keep the hunger. Moses didn't begin his ministry until he was 80. Abraham did not have Isaac until he was 100. David ran from Saul for seven years. If you get a Word today and it doesn't happen tomorrow, grow up. Calm down. It will come to pass when you're ready.

I am Joseph. His brothers were terrified. He initiated the power of self-identification. The most powerful thing that can happen to you is for you to finally realize who you are in Jesus Christ. Because then you can wait for what God is going to do, what people say about you doesn't matter. When you know who you are, your spiritual life changes, your prayer life changes, the way Satan comes at you changes. The moment we know who we are, all fear leaves. You come into a peace and joy that no one can take away from you and that is what Satan is most threatened by. The declaration of your identity in Christ is enough to change your life destiny and environment. When you recognize who you are in Jesus Christ, Satan can't threaten you and the dynamics of spiritual warfare change. When people look at their horoscopes they are looking for signs and affirmations because they don't know who they are. But when you know who you are, you are established. Men who don't know who they are live with low self-esteem. Women who don't know who they are think their body is their most valuable asset. Once you declare who you are in Jesus Christ you will operate differently and people around you will operate differently around you and the enemy will be threatened.

John 18:1: Throughout Jesus' life in ministry he waited until he went to Jerusalem because he had to arrive at an appointed time. He healed people who knew who he was and he could go to the cross because he knew who he was. When Jesus said, "I am he" the enemies fell to the ground. Circumstances in life will not be able to break you. You will have already defeated all that Satan will try to throw at you.

I am Joseph. I have a destiny on my life. I have a word that is going to pass. I have a relationship with God. Only God can tell you who you are in him.

Chapter 17
THE LARGER PURPOSE

Genesis 45:1-7

A few years ago I had a problem with some people who were vexing my Spirit. They made me feel my ministry was threatened and my future at MSBC uncertain. I called my spiritual leader and he laughed and said, "If you are required to drive 80 mph and the lives of others depend on it are you really going to take your eyes off the road and swat gnats?" What he was saying is, "Keep your eyes on the larger issues, the greater purpose." In this passage, Joseph is saying, "Look, I am your brother, how is my father doing?" He asked because his father poured into his life and was the symbol of his covenant relationship with God. Then very practically he says, "My father thinks I'm dead or living with a great deal of distress and I am living as the prince of Egypt." He just wanted his father to know that he was okay. He wanted the brothers to come close to him and recognize he was really their brother.

This is one of the high parts of the story because finally Joseph was able to explain to his brothers why God put him there. Now Joseph is rich. He is not only powerful and wealthy, but he is rich in God because he can stand in front of his enemies and betrayers and reconcile with them. He can release them from vengeance, restore them and speak into them. Money is not the only riches. We ought to go after things that have more redeeming and eternal values than paper money. At this moment in the story Joseph is a type of Savior, a type of Christ, because he went before them to save lives (cp. John 14). He disarmed his brothers, not scolding them or chastising them for selling him, but he explained to them the larger purpose.

I live for my "ah-ha" moments. These are the moments when the light comes on and I see what God is doing. The Bible is one tapestry and all the stories are woven together, so read the Bible long enough and you will see how it is connected. If you can't see the why of things in your life then there is no closure and you can't move on. Why do bad things happen to good people? Joseph would say, "God sent me before to save a generation of people." God made my life a scenario of his sovereign will and purpose. Closure is everything but we want to know why we are facing what we are facing or we can't go forward. But we have to obey and we may not get an answer until years later as to why. When the light finally comes on and makes sense "why" we went through what we did, that ah-ha moment is the answered prayer. You're walking, trying to do God's will, and wind up in a life or death situation, your very own lion's den. You ask God why and you get no answer. You come out scarred, then years later you find out why and God shows you that he not only heard you, he also answered your prayers. The Book of Revelation ends by bringing God's people into Heaven with him. All these things in Jesus Christ work toward our great future and successful end in God.

Joseph tells his brothers that this work was God's doing to save the race. You should not have a problem forgiving your enemies and those who are sent to destroy you, if their actions couldn't break you. If they couldn't break you, no matter what they did, what are you mad about? You ought to look back at them and think how they didn't break you, they made you stronger and brought you closer to the Lord. You have overcome tragedy, shame, and reproach, and you are still standing. Joseph tells his brothers, "Look, don't be upset because I didn't die in the pit."

The divine life is one that is lived from a God-focused perspective. That is why the Church exists, the Bible exists, and why we are here. Joseph's words were, "Don't be upset, you had very little to do with my being here. God brought me here to save your lives." When you are God-focused jealousy is removed, patience undergirds you and sorrow and suffering lead to hymns and psalms. People who are immature in the faith say everything is God. People who grow in the faith believe the same thing, but they don't always talk about. They know God was in it all. Remember, "Don't let your left hand know what your right hand is doing." Real spirituality is born in private and its fruit is public. Joseph shared with his brothers the larger purpose. The larger purpose says I can handle these things, going to prison, being hated, etc., because you don't take your eyes off the larger purpose. Focus on the larger purpose.

The key to understanding the larger purpose of things is gaining understanding. The grace of God on Joseph's life delays his brother's fears because he wanted his brothers to get the larger picture. The one who gains understanding moves from a place of victim to teacher. Have you ever met people who make the same mistake all the time, are always justifying their actions? They don't apologize because they do not possess understanding. Not everyone in church has un-derstanding. Joseph says don't be distressed by what you've done because God did this for a reason. When you have understanding you grow in mercy and mercy becomes the illustration of your Godliness. Others may not know why what happened to you happened because it will be your ministry to know why what happened to you happened. Anyone who goes through a storm in faith and comes out is a minister. You went through it to come out that you might be a living illustration and spokesperson on God's behalf. This may be to help someone else come through (2 Corinthians 1:3-4).

Understanding this is the ability to grasp the truth of reality and the mercies of God. If there is a car accident and two people run into each other, who wins if they get out and start fighting? The police come and ask the parties what happened and they blame each other, but understanding explains what happened. Understanding unties the knot; the ability to be objective about a situation, to see what it is, to call the truth of what it is and then resolve it in one's heart. To couples in an argument don't say, "You've been doing this for so long it makes me sick," instead say, "When you do this, this is how I feel." When you use your mouth as a weapon and attack your partner you are not being understanding. Understanding is recognizing that I am not always right and all the events of my life are not coincidence, but God's working in my life.

Understanding is a spiritual gift (Isaiah 11). The gift of understanding is revealed early in life. Understanding is the key to all visions, all dreams, and all revelations that come from the Holy Spirit (Daniel 2). The king brought all the scientific, esoteric, and cultural minds together and none of them could explain the dream. But Daniel received wisdom from God. When the Bible talks about wisdom and understanding it is talking about a very deep, spiritual concept (Matthew 13:13). Jesus says, "I can speak all day and you won't understand it." You can't repent unless you have understanding. "Though it cost you all you have, get understanding." [Proverbs 4:7] It is available to us.

Genesis 45:5-7: The reason why Joseph could speak kindly to his brothers is because God had given him understanding. Understanding gives you the ability to reconcile difficult situations and brings closure. It shows that God controls life's events and fulfills the purposes of his anointed. You are praying to be stronger as you go through something, but when you come out you will be stronger. If you are a child of God, you must have faith that God's timing is perfect. Intentions to annihilate you while you are in God will turn out to exalt you, i.e. everything the enemy does will raise you up in the eyes of God. It could be that your life/journey/experiences are a part of a much larger picture than you have ever considered. You, ordinary you, could actually be a part of a much larger work of the Spirit than you ever considered when you were in the storm. One germ can make the whole body sick and one person can affect the Kingdom of God. You don't want to stand before God as he tells you your life story and reveals all your unmet potential. WE are ordinary, common, and God is no respecter of persons, but at the same time we are instruments to be used by God to shape the lives of people in this era. The hand of God is behind the events of your life. This knowledge will bring you strength, peace, love, and courage. Our lives are the concern of angels and demons.

Satan meant it for evil. God meant it for good. Keep your eyes on the big picture, the great purposes, and the great things of God. If we keep our eyes on the larger picture, we will not forget that "we wrestle not against flesh and blood." It's not about the person coming after me. I can face Goliath and defeat him because it's about something larger. My friends can leave me, my loved ones can go away from me and it's okay because my eyes are on the larger picture.

Chapter 18
LIVING IN A NEW PLACE

Genesis 45:16-28 (take note of 24)

You cannot grow until you become empty. You cannot grow until you reach a spiritual crisis. Paul says he was given a thorn in the flesh that God would not remove to keep him humble. Then Paul says he learned to glory in his afflictions. Our best times with God will be those crises times, when we are removed from the day to day and brought before the throne in desperate need of help.

When a man or woman is dealing with God, and that includes reading the Bible and praying, you'll find what you read is a connection for what God is saying to you at the time. There is something inside us, maybe a part of human nature, but it is in our hearts and spirits—it's a terrible mistake—but we always look for an end. We want the story to end and the applause with the happy ending. The downside is if things don't go our way we look for an exit, in our marriages and jobs, friendships, etc. But in the scriptures we never come to an end. We come through seasons and changes, moving from a plateau to something else. We get to where Jacob and his family are living in Egypt and have lived there for a long time, but that is not the end of the story. We get to Exodus and the decedents are in bondage and a new season is starting. Instead of looking for an end we should look for instruction. That is far more important than trying to define where you are in God.

This message is about prosperity, but prosperity is a multifaceted thing with God. It is not confined to great wealth. When you find people who have material prosperity, ask them how much it cost.

Pharaoh rejoiced when heard about Joseph's brothers coming to Canaan. Pharaoh knew some of his story but he didn't know the entire story about how the brothers sold him to slavery. Pharaoh gave them the wealth of Egypt. In one afternoon, they went from living in famine and poverty to being very, very wealthy. They were brought from one place to a new place. Pharaoh's kindness and liberality show what type of leader he was. This was important because favor involves timing. You run into people with great power and influence, who see something in you and desire to invest into you. This man was wise, benevolent and even godly (compare him to the pharaoh in Exodus). It shows that he respected the wisdom God placed on Joseph.

Remember, if you want the Holy Spirit start in Proverbs and seek God's wisdom. Isaiah 11 talks about the seven manifestations of the Holy Spirit upon the Messiah and one of them is wisdom. What Pharaoh does for Joseph's brothers cannot be compared to what Joseph did in interpreting the dream and saving all of Egypt. Here, Pharaoh is a type of God. Joseph is a type of Christ. Because of Joseph, Pharaoh blesses all his family. It is because we are in Jesus Christ that God blesses us. Our relationship with God is due to our relationship with Jesus Christ.

Jacob's sons are given wealth as a sign that the family is moving into a new place. They are given prosperity. If you are praying for prosperity and not righteousness you are in error. Any ministry telling you about what you can get and not who you should become is leading you astray. It was who Joseph was that made these provisions for his family. There is a place in the Spirit of God where you do not want the wealth of the world because you would sacrifice the riches of your fellowship with God. Isaiah gave a word that healed the leper and denied the riches offered to him. But the servant was after the wealth and took the leprosy with it. If you are after the wealth you are after the snare, but if you are after the Lord you are after the liberty. When churches and individuals start going after things, the Lord says, "I love you. If only you could see what I have for you. I will wait while you go after these things until you are struck down."

As we seek God and come into the shift in the Spirit, we will come into prosperity. But what kind of prosperity will it be? For us it should not be a new car or house. It's not new clothing or more money in the bank. Prosperity should be your heart's desire, when the seeds sown began to grow, when your labor is rewarded or prayers have been answered. John 15 is prosperity. Ask what you will and you will receive, but if you abide in Jesus you will not ask certain things and pray reckless prayers because you will have the mind and heart of Christ. Our asking won't be a matter of what we retain, but who we are. Joseph was who he was, but he was ordained to go through trials that he might prosper and bring a nation into a new place. To the Josephs: Do not be discouraged about how hard and difficult life is for you, but soon the people that love you will come into a new place with you and with God. Instead of having money to pay the most expensive doctor wouldn't you rather be able to call on THE Doctor? The Joseph blessing is prosperity. But another word for prosperity is shalom, peace, wholeness, soundness, completeness. The women with an issue of blood spent all she had on doctors, and she touched Jesus in faith of healing. And Jesus said to her, "Go in peace because your faith has brought you prosperity." [Paraphrase mine: Mark 5.34] Your prosperity is that you have been made whole. When you come into knowledge of "you shall not want" from Psalm 23: 1, you come into prosperity. Isn't it interesting how money comes to people who don't need it? We know in our hearts you cannot measure blessing by the amount of what you have. God is your portion and that is enough. Here are some points to reflect upon regarding real prosperity:

When God brings you into a new place, a life of prosperity whatever it might be, you need instruction and direction because that new place will be foreign to you. Verses 16-19, Pharaoh gave the brothers instructions to receive prosperity. When God opens the windows of heaven for us, blessings chase blessings and we are not even prepared to receive them all.

When you move into a new place, your resources, your livelihood, and the people in your life will change drastically. With every stage of spiritual growth, there are people you leave behind and the same goes with prosperity. We are not thinking we are better than others but we cannot take them all with us. Abram had to leave his kin. Peter, Andrew, and John had to leave the fishing business. Whatever God is doing you will have to leave people, but God will bring new people and new circumstances. It's not a matter of being better than anyone but recognizing that every move of God we go alone. Verses 17 and 18 say you will have the best of Egypt but you must leave where you were and what you have been. You cannot stay in Canaan if you want to have this. If your prosperity is separate from your relationship with God it will always have a snare in it. You need hardships to grow. If your focus is on material things you will sabotage very vital lessons. It took 15 years to build the new sanctuary at Morning Star Baptist Church in Boston. (in 2004.) . One reason was there were very precious souls who didn't couldn't see the need for it. They served faithfully but could not imagine a multi-million dollar campaign. I patiently wait for God to speak to their hearts. Their faith was not strong enough for such an undertaking. If any opportunities come to you that you must destroy others to get, then it is not God. When you read about prosperity in the Old Testament, the children of Israel are the focus and for them it is obedience to God, possession of their land, and peace and prosperity. But in the New Testament it says "blessed are the poor in spirit, blessed are those who mourn…" Jesus says if you want my blessing and favor you must deny yourself and take up your cross. You must bear things beyond your comprehension. Character is built through suffering.

Satan stands in front of God and God offers to put Job up for Satan's test. God knows in all that Satan will try to put him through Job will not lose his prosperity. Come to Morning Star because you are trying to grow and become more Christ-like. Prosperity is out of our relationship with Jesus Christ. Therefore our central blessing is not the inheritance of a plot of land in Palestine or a high paying job in North America. Our blessing centers on our adoption with God and our gift of eternal life. Prosperity is knowing whether or not you are saved. Consider prosperity a season, and if you are going to know when God is blessing versus when he is saying "wait don't move," it will be because you have such a relationship with God that is so sensitive even if others are moving forward you will discern to wait because of where God is with you. Your prosperity is *your* prosperity and it is unique to your relationship with God.

Verse 24, Joseph was telling his brothers, "Don't spend your time fighting about what happened in the past, thank God for where you are **now**." You are in a new season and a different place now. In Nehemiah 8, the people were coming out of 70 years of slavery and finally, with the walls built, had a semblance of their identity. And Ezra opened the Scriptures and read them to the people and the people wept because of the conviction; but instead of weeping and crying, recognize that we are coming into a sacred place in God. "Do not grieve for the joy of the Lord is your strength." [Nehamiah 8:10] This is the same tone Joseph speaks to his brothers. Don't argue, but recognize you are in a new place; share, eat the fat, and rejoice in the Lord. This is what God is doing right here, right now. And with great conviction will come great joy and prosperity because we will not be focused on materialism but on God and our relationship with Jesus Christ.

This season of great blessing and favor will require great sacrifice and prayer. Men and women will come into sanctuaries and before the service even starts they will feel conviction and healing from the anointing. Relationships will be restored, people will be called to the work of the ministry, and spiritual warfare will occur; but people will not be afraid.

Heavenly Father, prepare my heart and soul to live in a new place.

Chapter 19
MOVING TO GOSHEN

Genesis 46, emphasis 34

We have a hunger for the Lord that He put there. We have visions and dreams of our life with God and spirituality. Our feet are on the ground and we deal with the flesh but our heart seeks deeper things in God and we deal with the conflict constantly. We face on a daily basis that the situation around us contribute to who we are and we hope that instead of allowing our situation to dictate who we are and how we were perceived, we would be perceived by who we are on the inside and let that dictate the situation. The force of spirituality is being who we are on the inside even though our situation denies it.

There were times when we didn't care and we just fit God in. But now the prayer is, "Lord, what do you want and how do I arrive?" Pray for the pastor's message on repentance and on the question, "How do we become our prayer?" where repentance is final and we don't have to go back down that route in our life. With all the people who claim to have gifts and callings, those whom God actually uses are very small in number. The rest God tolerates and we tolerate.

"The harvest is plentiful, but the laborers are few" [Matthew 9:37] and they are precious to God because he doesn't have many that fit the criteria. When a man or woman develops in the Spirit that person gives their lives to the Lord. They have to be available to whatever God wants to do because not everyone will reach a point of sacrifice where they will do whatever He wants to do. When we ask God to be used we must be prepared to let God move us however, whenever, to bring us trials and turmoil, and to endure great spiritual sacrifice. Change becomes the constant. The church bucks against this because the church thinks constancy is security. Change becomes the constant for the servant and the lack of change becomes the death of the church. The key to ministry is to discern what will be best and what will cause death. The pastor is not the best speaker, nor the best prayer, but the one called to lead the congregation.

God, you're telling me my next move involves promotion and is in Your will, yet the next move in my life is a place where no one will like me? Where I will face more conflict than I felt before the move? You are sending me to Goshen (verse 34)? The Lord says, "Prepare yourself to be in my shelter, in a hostile environment." God is moving us one by one to a deeper spirituality in order to be more effective but when we move there we will face a different set of enemies and challenges. They will be magnified and the stakes will be higher, but we will be built up in the process. When you become the instrument of God change becomes constant and it is important to make a decision to detach yourself from the values and people that you found comfort in so you can be unencumbered. The thing that will hold us back will be the thing that brought us there. God is not in what we had, God is current and present; and with what he is doing next we will not be able to rely on the things we found safety and comfort in.

We thank God for what he is doing in our life at this time. We learned to pray and grow and have developed at this time. We sense God calling us somewhere new, but are so comfortable with what we have at this time and not sure about the future, so we hold on. But what we hold on to dies, especially when God has already shifted. Genesis 45 ends with Jacob deciding to leave his present and walk to his future. Before he does he brings a sacrifice to God, thanking Him for what he has done at this time. However we move we have to pray, "God, I thank you for where I've been!" But then we have to pack our bags and move to the next place in God. Genesis 46:1 says, "Israel set out with all that was his." His providential divinely purposed name, under the inspiration of the Holy Spirit, to the place that God was taking him with everything that he could take. We can't take everything when we move, only the things which God has given us permission to take. To live in the Spirit we must understand that we must be adaptable and recognize that every relationship that we have is in God and when they must end it is okay.

The revival and the shift are about names. Every person who is about a shift in the Spirit, God has assigned. He has a record of every single name that is a part of the Spirit of God in the fellowship. Remember the days and the years that we named the theme, the shift, and these stories, because we will look back at this time and see what God has done in the Spirit in our lives. We are moving into spiritual history in this church. These names weren't written during the move… they were written after the fact. The miracles that Jesus did weren't written at that moment they were written after the fact. We will realize, after the fact, that something great happened and we were a part of it. We are approaching something that requires us to pray and seek God like we never have before. We are approaching Azusa. Seventy names are mentioned. Seven is the number of completion. Seventy names represent the nations. Remember that the Egyptians don't like shepherds.

Chapter 20
STAGES OF BLESSING

Genesis 47:7-10

Imagine that moment when Jacob realizes his son is alive and well and able to provide for the family. There is something in Jacob that blesses Pharaoh. Pharaoh seems to have all that anyone would need on earth and yet Jacob blesses Pharaoh. There is a blessing on your life. That is not to mean you live in some false biblical utopia where nothing goes wrong. The blessing is that the saints will end well, even if it is on the stake. The pilgrimage of the saints is the same. Pharaoh asked Jacob, "How old are you?" and Jacob responded, "My *pilgrimage* was 130 years, hard and difficult, and yet not as long as my fathers." His life had been difficult and yet he blesses Pharaoh.

God's servants go through different stages: blessing or the announcement of blessing, estrangement, brokenness, desperation, fulfillment, and exultation. If God makes a promise to you, if something suddenly good happens to you, the thing that will happen next is estrangement. The Spirit of God fell on Jesus and he went to the Wilderness. Joseph was given a dream from God and then separated from his family. Paul met Jesus on the road to Damascus, but he felt estrangement because the Jewish people saw him as a traitor and Christians were fearful because he persecuted them. When you go through estrangement your dreams are grey, you walk around with melancholy and you feel like brass wondering if God is hearing your prayers yet you are in the palms of the hands of the master. You can't see it or feel it, not realizing you are there, and you go through a period of brokenness. At the moment of desperation your faith is tried in the furnace and purified to become more precious than gold and never again lost. Then fulfillment comes. The fulfillment is saying, "Lord, whatever happens I'm alright." That's where the promotion comes. Not because you are anointed, gifted, or talented. It's when you say it doesn't matter. Everyone must go through that and everyone's story is different.

The path of Joseph is the path of Jacob. The path of Jacob is the path of Abraham. The path of Abraham is the path of Israel. The path of Israel is the path of Jesus. Joseph finds himself in Egypt—so does Jesus. Do you recognize that your detour is God's will? Your brick wall is God's will. The thing that hurts about hitting a brick wall is you usually hit it at full speed. But that is God's will for you. In Genesis 12:10-20 Abram went down to Egypt because of famine in the land. Egypt becomes the vital part of Israel's future. In Matthew 2:13 and Hosea 11:1 the Messiah had to be called out of Egypt because Abram was called out of Egypt, and Jacob was called out of Egypt, and Israel was called out of Egypt. Every single one of us was called out of Egypt in a metaphorical sense. We were making bricks without straw and we heard a voice in the bush saying, "Come out!"

Joseph presents his father to Pharaoh and Jacob bows down and not only greets him but blesses him. This is a man who almost lost his son, lived in poverty because of the famine, had to move his whole clan to a land God had not promised him, forcing him to move to a land and a country that was not their own, but he has the conscious to bless Pharaoh. It was a salutation but the Bible says it was a blessing. What was in him? Jacob had something in him that Pharaoh did not have. He blessed him because he had a relationship with Jehovah. He blessed the King of Egypt. What did he say? Maybe he said to himself that because he is the son of promise he recognizes he is in the will of God and he has God's grace on his life. He can pray that the grace also rests on Pharaoh. When there is a blessing on your life it does not leave. You can fall and not lose it. You can be sick and not lose it.

What does it mean to have a blessing on your life?

The Lord is with you always. We don't pray that much and when we do we wait for a conscious something, but the Lord is always with us.

Your path is divinely ordained. Don't be jealous of anyone else.

God is the ultimate provider. He will be there. God will make you hungry; he will hold back because you may need more than a piece of bread on a given day. You may need faith or trust. If you are the elect of God never doubt your needs will be meet even if you have to suffer.

You are aware of God's presence. The inner man gets quiet. You are not concerned about what man is going to do to you or what is going on around you.

Nothing can destroy you. Nothing Joseph went through could destroy him. Nothing Paul went through could destroy him. Nothing Jesus went through could destroy him.

The Lord will bring people into your path to bless you. Trust God and people will do you favors and they won't know why. When you least expect it people will pour into you.

You have reached a point of spirituality where you leave a blessing with people. The Bible says when you go into the good man's house you leave a blessing. When you grow in God you will go to the store and pray for people you see. You don't need money; you need relationships. If you have relationships you will have whatever resources you need, as a result of the relationships. Joseph gets in relationship with Pharaoh and Pharaoh brings Jacob's whole family there.

We get invited in the room because of God. The rich and powerful have the money and the resources but what they want is God. He is what they don't have. There is a blessing on my life and I can be assured that I can leave people with a blessing.

Chapter 21
HARD TIMES, HARD DECISIONS AND HARD LEADERSHIP

Genesis 47:13-31, emphasis 27

Imagine: The people had to give up their money, their livestock, their land, and their lives to Pharaoh, just to eat. Joseph had the seed but he didn't give it to them. Yet, they thanked him.

The scripture starts out by saying, "There was no food." Joseph was credited for saving both Egypt and Canaan from starvation and increasing the power of Pharaoh, but he was still not seen in a great light. He could have given the seed away but he didn't. The principle is that some decisions we make can have far-reaching effects into the future. The spiritual life is about one thing and that is the point. Sometimes one thing can change everything for better or for worse. David, sitting at home, told the captain to number the army. It was only one thing. But that one thing showed his distrust of God and 70,000 people suffered. All Moses did was smite the rod, one thing, and it kept him out of The Promised Land of Canaan. We have to guard our lives because we never know what that one thing is.

The writers of Genesis place this event in a peculiar place. Before this we saw Jacob meeting Pharaoh, blessing him, and Pharaoh making promises to Jacob. Then the next verse says, "There was no food." No food. Joseph is there. Egypt is a land of plenty. Jacob is there. WE don't end on a high note, but a low note. There is no food. Why is this important? Because God **said** that would be the case. If God tells you something is coming and you don't prepare for that thing, then you have the right to suffer the consequences of that thing you were unprepared for prophetically. The numbers of earthquakes of high devastation have increased, but did not Jesus say things would describe the time? The body of Christ today must be able to discern prophetically. They need praxis to be able to discern what's going on in the world. There are hard times coming ahead and the saints of God will need a theology and a worship that will help them through. If the grace of God increases on your life in this year it will increase because the conditions on our life will be more perilous. We are living in the ethos of anger. Anger and rebellion are the order of the day.

When you think about the fact that there was no food in Egypt you must go back to Pharaoh's dream and Joseph's interpretation. The prophecy of hard times came to Egypt. The "theology" of always having the blessings of God as a sign of His favor has a short shelf life. Money has wings. This part of Joseph's story represents the time where prophecy is needed in the church. As prophecy is emphasized, false prophecy will also be emphasized. While Paul was in prison people were preaching Christ, "out of selfish ambition rather than from pure motives." [Philippians 1:18] There are people in the ministry that are not of God. "Why would Satan not do that? Why would he not sow tares with the wheat?" Don't set yourself up to be deceived. There is a need for prophecy but we must be careful of false prophecy. Joseph heard from God and was on top during hard times. 2 Chronicles 20:20: Trust in God and in his oracles, 1 Thessalonians 5:20: Do not treat prophecy in contempt, Revelation 1:1: Blessed in the one who hears and reads the words of this prophecy. Prophecy is important to the body of Christ, important in the last days, and important to the Shift; we only must be careful.

The desperation of the region at this time in Egypt and Canaan cannot be overstated. It was so bad in Egypt. The people took all their valuable possessions and sold them. Then they sold all their livestock. Then they sold all their land. They were still hungry. Then they sold their freedom. They were still hungry. Joseph gave them seed and they praised God for seed, not even bread. In the moment they became slaves they received seed. The principle is this: In God, if you are called upon to go lower than low, when you arrive there you will be given the seeds to your future prosperity and blessing. No Child of God who hits rock bottom stays there. If you hit rock bottom out of Christ you don't have the attitude to handle it. When you are in the Lord you are in the cocoon of his grace. If you are prophetic in your life and operate under the unction of the Holy Spirit, the word that you speak sometimes will bring hardship on your own life. Elijah said it would not rain for three years; then Elijah got hungry. His brook dried up in the will of God. The Lord didn't save you for an easy life, he saved you to be in him.

They sell their land and their lives. When you give your life to Jesus Christ He becomes your owner. And He does what He pleases with your possessions.

He allows you to be a steward. They became Pharaoh's property and Joseph gave them permission to administer on the land they no longer owned. When you purchase the pearl of great price God gives it back to you but it is no longer yours.

To receive this salvation we must give our income, our family, our life, and our future. But when we do, and the Lord gives it back, it's better than what we had before. But we can't go on unless we give it to him.

The people thanked Joseph for saving their lives even though Joseph placed them in servitude. The times were so hard it took the kind of leadership Joseph could offer just for the people to survive.

At the end of the story Jacob is old and asks his son to bury him in the promised land of Canaan. They were given the best land in Goshen but they were not home in Goshen. We are in the world but not of the world. We pay our taxes but we are not home down here. You can't settle down in Egypt. If you like Egypt too much, you will not prepare yourself for going home. Jacob is saying, "You should never be too content in this world and where you are." You ought not to make the circumstances your home. You ought not to hold on to a ministry such that you can't leave it and they can't call on someone else. There ought to be some discontent in all the things that are going on. God wants to heal you from the inside out by making known there is some discontent in all of us. Why? It's simply because we don't need to be buried in Egypt.

Chapter 22
THE FATHER'S BENEDICTION

Genesis 48

Ephesians 1:3 "Blessed be the God and Father of our Lord Jesus Christ, who has blessed us with every spiritual blessing in the heavenly places in Christ…"

In the Old Testament blessings were passed down from generation to generation. Before Joseph's father Jacob died, he requested the presence of his grandsons born to Joseph in Egypt. He was about to die, old and decrepit; but with all the strength he had, he rose up and told Joseph about the story of God blessing him and of losing his wife Rachel. He wanted to bless the grandsons. This is a very tender moment. Joseph thought he would never see his father again but he was able and also able to provide for him. Joseph was very austere and rich yet he prostrated himself before his father. Every nation other than America honors the aged. We honor the strong and the young. We don't honor the people who walked with God and have lived long lives. Don't believe you will be anything in God and dishonor the elderly. Honor their witness and testimony and experience. It is important to recognize in the Spirit and in your life.

Joseph had two sons in Egypt. The first was Ephraim and the second was Manasseh. The name Ephraim means *doubly fruitful* and Manasseh means *causing me to forget*. This showed Joseph recognized the seasons he was in. Some people may be uncomfortable with what is going on in their lives because they have not settled down in the season. Don't worry about where you are just ask God to declare to your spirit what season you are in. Jesus preached for three years for his ministry. The first year was popularity, the second adversity, and the third persecution. But he knew what he was to face.

The father's blessing is very important. Abraham became the father of monotheism. Although there is no specific reference of Abraham passing a blessing to Isaac, we know from context that he passed down a blessing in two ways. First, when God spared Isaac on Mount Moriah. Abraham took Isaac into his arms and embraced him, blessing him and thanking God for sparing him. Second, in Genesis 24 Abraham requires one of his servants to find a wife for Isaac and has him make a vow that the wife will not come from the Gentile women. You can be unequally yoked whenever you meet a man or woman that does not share the same intensity for God that you do. When you meet the daughter or son of your tribe, when the difficulties come—and they will inevitably come—you have a sense of agreement that the covenant and Spirit is the same. Otherwise you throw the locks in the air and wait to see how they will come down. Before you give a man or woman your body, let them show you their spirit. People talk a good game but make sure you see them on their knees and reading scripture and living in the consecration of God's Spirit on their lives. You want to marry someone who has a heart for God, a heart for you, and is healed enough that they will not use you as a tool to becoming a whole person. If they try to use you they will break you. God will teach you how to love as he loves. Abraham did implicitly bless God; He sought God's will for his life.

When Abraham was old and ready to give the blessing Jacob came in to steal it. And when Esau came he could not receive it because the father can only give the Father's blessing once. What is the Father's blessing? It's **the passing of God's favor** to the next generation. It's the **passing of the covenant** relationship that the father had with God. How can that be so? We don't know. But when Abraham passed a blessing to his son God confirmed what Abraham did and allowed the covenant relationship that he had go to his son, and his son's son. It is also the **passing of the prophecy** of God over the life. The father can see things in the children that the children cannot see.

Jacob said to Joseph, "From now on they [Joseph's two sons] are mine." Then he embraced them and kissed them. Jacob adopted Joseph's son as his own offspring. In essence he said these boys will be as your brothers. Everything that is mine will be theirs. "Don't forget about God's adopted sons and daughters! We have been adopted! Ezekiel 18:16-18, "God picked us up out of the trash and told us to live!" In Romans 8:15, "Upon our lives is the Spirit of adoption. We are heirs of God and joint heirs with Jesus Christ." Whatever God has given to the son, he has given to us! Manasseh is mentioned as a tribe in Revelation and Ephraim is the name of one of the gates in the city of Jerusalem. God made his name a gate in Jerusalem.

Your heavenly Father has adopted you. You have a relationship of adoption with your Heavenly Father. You are a part of the family with Abraham, Isaac, Jacob, the prophets, Jesus, and the righteous. If you ever feel lonely or insignificant remember you have the blessing of the Father on your life.

Chapter 23
THE SOVEREIGNTY
OF GOD

Our Christianity does not come in a box marked "fragile." God knows about all the drama we will ever experience still the love of God through Jesus Christ is constant.

There is a tension between contentment and discontentment in the Spiritual life. If you sway too far one way your contentment will keep you from striving from anything. If you swing too far the other way, your discontentment will keep you blinded from the will of God. There is a balance. Wherever you are right now, ask God not to change things. Do not resent the life you have and attempt to replace it. Salvation equals outcome. The theme of the Jewish-Christian revelation is about outcome. In Genesis we are estranged from God by sin. In Revelation we are brought into fellowship again. Jesus starts his ministry with concern about outcome. When he asks his disciples who he is and Peter answers, he begins to teach them of how he must be purged, killed, and rise again. He was teaching them about outcome. God sees us how we should be in Jesus Christ. The problem in the Church is that we are not teaching about outcome enough. If we did then we would not feel so bad when we stumble. We would recognize the outcome is set. WE are not, of all people, most miserable because we are tethered to the hope of the outcome of our lives with Jesus Christ. Joseph said don't be upset with the outcome of my life—you meant it for evil, but God meant it for good.

The Spirit of God that was on Joseph did not end with Joseph but rests on all those who are the kindred of Joseph in this present time. Do not resent your life because it is hard, keep your eye on the outcome. Joseph's life was called to be difficult. God is the author of a play called "The Story of the Human Species." There is a cast of characters, some who have it easy and some who have it difficult. They both have their purpose, so those who have it difficult should not complain or resent those who have it easy. Those who have it easy could not *take* what you have to take. He made you to bear the difficulty now because he knows the outcome is not only glorious here and now, but it is glorious in the hereafter. Someone walks in the church and their lives are a wreck and you try to decide whether or not you want them to sit beside you, don't do that because you don't know the outcome yet. The outcome that God designs for you is different than your story.

Verse 20 is the conclusion of the words of Joseph, the reason this whole story was written. The people with the Joseph Blessing on their lives are graced with the favor of God to provide, support, and influence a great number of people. All the influence, recognition, and authority society gives a person does not come from your education but from a grace higher than that—the Joseph Anointing. You are meant to influence others far beyond your understanding so your life has to be hard because God has to bring out the truth of who you are to other people. The truth of who you are will minister to people without you saying a word. The events of Joseph's life were all destined by God, and God shaped Joseph's life by providence.

Joseph has a dream that leads to rejection from his brothers and is almost killed by them. He is sold to slavery, accused falsely, only to come out and interpret Pharaoh's dream. He is made second over all of Egypt and he becomes the savior of Egypt and Canaan. Joseph does not live with regret. He does not spend his time saying, "I wish I could have" or "I should have done this/that." He does not live there anymore. He doesn't regret what happened because God meant it for Joseph's good. All of Joseph's experiences were part of a tapestry that God designed for his story. All of Joseph's skills were a result of his relationship with God, which he did not understand. His ability to suffer is divine, his wisdom God given, and his gifts anointed and irrevocable. For every person who comes to Jesus Christ as Lord and Savior had a relationship with God before. When you finally come to terms with who you are in Jesus Christ, it is only the recognition of who you were. Sin could not destroy you. Everything Joseph went through was a result of his relationship with God. God is not fair; God is awesome.

Samuel went to anoint the king. And all those came out who looked like kings. But the boy who was rejected by his own father was chosen by the Father to be king before he even met Samuel.

In Genesis 41:39, 40, Joseph has knowledge that everything he has, everything he will be, is a result of his relationship with God which he does not understand. In Genesis 41:45 Pharaoh gave Joseph the name Tsaphnath-Paenéach, which means "God speaks and God lives." This is the shift. You don't wait for Sunday morning but you live a life where God speaks and God lives. You let God become the reality and divine power in your life. You recognize that your life is God directed and you do not lose sight of that. You never take your eyes off the truth that all things are working together for your good. Not just some things. This includes times of failure, sickness, hunger, loneliness and despair, when you are a thousand miles away from God. Even when your soul feels like a desert and hope left the stage. Whether you are in the pit, in the prison, or in the palace—all things work together for your good.

Joseph is a giant. Joseph has an unsettling inside himself that he is royalty. Joseph knows that God is no respecter of persons. Joseph is a giant spiritually, strategically, and socially in terms of the anointing and it took all these things which Joseph went through for his family to recognize Joseph as a giant of destiny. Joseph as a royal priesthood. Joseph has more than the rest he just has to discover how to mine it out. Single, lonely, in pain, broke; Joseph is a giant in God. He always was. Everyone seemed to know it. God called Joseph to such a place that others would bow down to him. Joseph is a giant. Over the lives of a multitude, Joseph becomes a gateway of prosperity and a conduit of blessing for everyone connected to him.

Even when you have momentary encounters with people, God will stamp them with favor and grace because they came into your presence. Joseph influences people. Joseph influences situations just by being there. Joseph cannot be stingy, or hoard, or be cheap, because Joseph's role is to provide for people. Joseph cannot be insecure about his gifts because he must use those gifts to bless others, even when he is not feeling blessed. Joseph understands that he lives in the Kingdom so he cannot lose anything because everything that Joseph receives is through the Kingdom of God. Joseph says "you meant it for evil; God meant it for good to bring me where I am today, so that I might provide for you." He provided for the men who were jealous of him and tried to kill him. Joseph is a giant.

Joseph cannot afford to be unforgiving. Joseph has to let everything go. Joseph cannot hold onto any injustice done to him because it will blind him from the grace of God. Joseph forgives because he knows that those who hurt him didn't understand the context of his life and they didn't understand who he was. Otherwise they would ask Joseph to pour into their lives. Because they weren't given the wisdom they did what they thought was best to make themselves secure but Joseph forgives because they were blind about his role in the future. Joseph does not have the option of being unforgiving. He can't because the people who created the injustice, and did the harm, were the instruments of God who chiseled the character that he would need to take the lofty place in God.

Thank God for every one of them because they make you who you are. Joseph is wired to be equipped for trouble. When trouble hits, Joseph knows what to do. Joseph does not panic or run. Joseph is the one that everyone brings their problems to and no one takes Joseph's problems because they are not wired or equipped to handle the trouble that he can handle. Some people have to take the lead when times get hard. That is the way He made you, Joseph. You cannot go into the future complaining and resentful that you have to be the one always taking the lead because that is the anointing and blessing of Joseph. Joseph says to his brothers that this was to save them. God called him to not only forgive, but also to save and provide for his persecutors and their children. We think we are doing a lot when someone breaks our hearts and we say, "I forgive you, don't do it again." Joseph says, "You tried to kill me, but I will forgive you, save you, provide for you and your children." That is how large the Joseph Blessing is.

Joseph is invaluable. He is the divine connector. He is the manifestation of wisdom. Joseph is the strategic key to everything God will do in a given family, at a given time and place. Joseph provides favor to people who don't deserve it, the voice of God to people who don't understand His role in their lives. God put something in Joseph to survive. Joseph cannot be broken. Hardships led Joseph to the high planes of God.

You are Joseph. So stop resenting where you are. Let go of unforgiveness. You are equipped to handle more, to carry more, to believe more than everyone around you. You are a general in God's army -- the leader of the choir, the captain of the team.

Problems find you. Troubles follow you. And destiny waits for you. Hold your head up. Walk into your destiny like a champion. You will never fail because you are the recipient of the most Unlikely Blessings.